Y0-BEZ-747

AN EFFECTIVE SCHOOLS PRIMER

AMERICAN ASSOCIATION OF SCHOOL ADMINISTRATORS

WITHDRAWN
HIEBERT LIBRARY
FRESNO PACIFIC UNIV.-M. B. SEMINARY
FRESNO. CA 93702

CONTENTS

TABLE OF CONTENTS

INTRODUCTION

Purpose of this Book

Over the past two decades, hundreds of school systems have put into practice a body of research and school improvement strategies commonly known as "Effective Schools." According to the pioneers of the effective schools movement, every school can improve the quality of education for all its students, including poor and minority children, by taking concrete steps to incorporate a set of characteristics identified by research as being present and essential in schools with successful track records.

One such characteristic is strong leadership—particularly at the principal level, but also at the superintendent and central office level. This finding alone speaks to the need for a publication that can help school administrators understand the effective schools process and, if they choose, implement it in their own districts. That is what this publication seeks to do.

In lay language, this publication sketches out the basic concepts of the effective schools movement as it has developed over time and discusses how it has been applied and refined in school settings around the country.

Organization of the Book

The book is divided into nine chapters. Chapter 1 presents an overview of the effective schools concept, describes its history and evolution, and discusses the basic characteristics, or "correlates," that are central to the effective schools process. Each of Chapters 2 through 7 takes one of six commonly agreed-on effective schools correlates and explains it in detail, using examples and commentary from researchers, school administrators, curriculum coordinators, university professors, and others. Chapter 8 discusses some procedures for implementing an effective schools process; and Chapter 9 reviews emerging trends in effective schools and school improvement research and development, and suggests some areas for further research.

Sources

The information in this publication has been culled from a range of primary sources, including hundreds of books, reports, monographs, studies, research presentations, and interviews with researchers and practitioners. Of particular help were the findings of two surveys of school administrators conducted by the American Association of School Administrators especially for this publication; as well as surveys and studies carried out by the U.S. General Accounting Office, the Center for Research in Elementary and Middle Schools at Johns Hopkins University, and the National Center for Effective Schools Research at the University of Wisconsin, Madison. The particular sources for each chapter are listed at the end of that chapter.

CHAPTER 1: OVERVIEW

"The fact that some schools have become effective in teaching the basic skills (and I suspect, in achieving many of the other desirable outcomes that we seldom measure) is evidence that it can be done."

—Wilbur Brookover

What are "Effective Schools"?

The body of research and practices commonly called "effective schools" has been a significant force in education reform during the past two decades—perhaps the most significant force for improving teaching and learning for disadvantaged and minority children. Thousands of schools throughout the country have implemented the effective schools process (and it is a process, not a program—a key distinction), often with district or state encouragement and sometimes under different names. New York State's effort, for example, is called the "Comprehensive School Improvement Program." The process piloted in six Western states by the Northwest Regional Educational Laboratory is called the "Onward to Excellence Movement." Other efforts are called simply "effective schools programs" or "school improvement programs."

Regardless of what they are called or how they have been modified to address local needs, effective schools efforts are based on some fundamental beliefs:

- That schools have the capacity to provide a quality education for all children, regardless of family background and social context;

- That schools with successful records of educating children from all backgrounds, especially disadvantaged ones, share certain

3

essential characteristics—most often relating to leadership, school climate, high expectations, instructional emphasis, educational assessment, and community involvement—which can be identified through careful research and replicated by other schools; and

- That any school can improve the quality of teaching and learning by making a concerted, building-wide effort to embody these essential characteristics.

From these core beliefs has emerged the variety of approaches and practices now widely recognized as the effective schools concept. The concept has been debated and refined over two decades and continues to be adapted to new grade levels and settings. Although the formative research was done in urban elementary schools, the resulting ideas can be applied in levels preschool through grade 12, and in all types of schools, regardless of size, geographic location, or socioeconomic setting. Moreover, any program, approach, method, or idea worth trying in a classroom can be incorporated into an effective schools model.

The effective schools process, by its very name, is evolutionary

A means, not an end. Flexibility and change, in fact, are central to the effective schools philosophy. As proponents of effective schools take care to stress, the effective schools concept is not a program, but a *process* into which other programs can be installed. The way the guiding researchers envisioned it, the process could be used to change curriculum, textbooks, instructional approaches, and any other areas requiring improvement. Lawrence Lezotte of Michigan State University, a major spokesperson of the effective schools movement and a collaborator on some of the seminal research, constantly reminds educators that "the effective schools process, by its very name, is evolutionary."

However a school approaches the process, its end goals—and the standards by which its success is evaluated—are the same: quality and equity. "[A] quality standard assures that the achievement level in a school is high," says Barbara O. Taylor, associate director of the National Center for Effective Schools at the University of Wisconsin at Madison. "[A]n equity standard assures that the high achievement does not vary significantly across a school's student population by socioeconomic status, race, ethnicity or gender."

History of the Effective Schools Movement

The Early Years: Reactions to Coleman

What we know as the effective schools concept is the brain-child of a core group of researchers who, during the late 1960s, began testing their ideas about child development in selected urban elementary schools serving mostly poor and minority children. To a notable extent, these researchers were motivated by a controversial report entitled *Equality of Educational Opportunity*, written by University of Chicago sociologist James S. Coleman. In this 1966 study, better known as the "Coleman Report," the author argued that schools make little difference in the lives of children and that a child's family background and general social context were far more important determinants of educational achievement. Coleman's findings triggered heated debate, and several researchers set out to disprove his conclusions. (An interesting footnote: Coleman ultimately revised his thinking in a second report some 15 years later, after a body of effective schools research had documented the impact that schools could make in the lives of poor and minority children.)

Comer and Weber: Schools Can Make a Difference

One researcher who took on Coleman was Dr. James Comer, a Yale psychiatrist and director of the university's Child Study Center. Comer believed that schools could do better with minority and poor children if they tended first to their psychological and social needs. In an effort to test his hypotheses in schools serving poor neighborhoods, Comer began a project, using a mental health approach, in two New Haven public elementary schools. Within three years, Comer noticed improvements in learning and parent participation in the pilot schools.

Another pioneer was George Weber, a New York City researcher, who in 1971 studied four urban elementary schools, selected because they provided effective instruction to children from poor neighborhoods. Weber found that all four schools shared some important characteristics:

- Strong leadership—the principal set the tone of the school, helped decide the instructional strategies, and organized and distributed the school's resources in a sound manner.

- High expectations for all students (which, although absolutely necessary was not by itself sufficient, Weber cautioned);

- An orderly, relatively quiet and pleasant atmosphere; and

- An emphasis on pupil acquisition of reading skills, reinforced through "careful and frequent evaluation of pupil progress."

Edmonds: The Five Basic Correlates

Weber's findings piqued the interest of the late Ronald Edmonds, then an assistant superintendent with the Michigan Department of Education, who later became a leader in the effective schools movement. Working with Lawrence Lezotte and Wilbur Brookover of Michigan State University, Edmonds set about applying Weber's concepts (which came to be known as correlates) in Detroit and 21 other Michigan school districts. After three years, Edmonds, Lezotte, and Brookover reported some signs of success. Edmonds transplanted the effort to New York City, where he implemented it in several additional elementary schools.

In 1979, while a lecturer and research project director at Harvard University, Edmonds spelled out his ideas in a paper, entitled "Effective Schools for the Urban Poor." This paper helped lay the foundation of what would become the effective schools movement. According the Edmonds, "the large differences in performance between effective and ineffective schools could not be . . . attributed to differences in the social class and family background of pupils enrolled in schools." Rather, he wrote, "the popularity of that belief continues partly because many social scientists and opinion makers continue to espouse the belief that family background is the chief cause of the quality of pupil performance. Such a belief has the effect of absolving educators of their professional responsibility to be instructionally effective."

Edmonds ended his 1979 remarks with three declarations that have since become a sort of rallying cry for the effective schools movement:

- "We can, whenever and wherever we choose, successfully teach all children whose schooling is of interest to us."

- "We already know more than we need to do that."

• "Whether or not we do it must finally depend on how we feel about the fact that we haven't so far."

Building upon Weber's research and his own work he had done with Lezotte and Brookover, Edmonds came up with his personal set of five characteristics, often called "correlates," of effective schools.

In recent years, parental and community involvement has come to be accepted as an indispensable sixth correlate to Edmonds original five.

Developing a Workable Group of Correlates

In reflecting on the history of the movement he helped spawn, Lawrence Lezotte said, "We will find that the '80s have laid the groundwork for real reform." A quick review of research conducted during the 1980s bears this out. During this decade, several prominent education researchers elaborated on the effective schools concept and correlates and moved from merely describing what constituted a more effective school toward developing approaches for implementation. The ultimate goal of this phase of research was to develop a process that could be used in a range of schools.

Ronald Edmonds'
Five Correlates of Effective Schools [sic]

1. Strong administrative leadership.
2. A climate of expectation in which no children are permitted to fall below minimum but efficacious levels of achievement.
3. The school's atmosphere is orderly but not rigid, quiet without being oppressive, and generally conducive to the business at hand.
4. Effective schools get that way partly by making it clear that pupil acquisition of basic skills takes precedence over all other school activities.
5. The principal and teachers must be constantly aware of pupil progress toward the instructional objectives through frequent testing.

Purkey and Smith: Away from Simplistic Recipes

In 1983, Stewart Purkey and Marshall Smith, then at the University of Wisconsin at Madison, reviewed the past research and, as they wrote, found it "weak in many respects, most notably in its tendency to present narrow, often simplistic, recipes for school improvement derived from non-experimental data." Acknowledging, however, that "theory and common sense support many of the findings of school effectiveness research," Purkey and Smith came up with their own set of "Thirteen Characteristics of Effective Schools." According to the two researchers, 9 of the 13 characteristics were essential to set the stage for school improvement: (1) school site management; (2) leadership; (3) staff stability; (4) curriculum articulation and organization; (5) staff development; (6) parental involvement and support; (7) school-wide recognition of academic success; (8) maximized learning time; and (9) district support from the central office. The remaining four were what Purkey and Smith called "process variables," meaning that they "constitute the dynamics of the school's culture and seem responsible for an atmosphere that leads to increased student achievement." These process variables include: (1) a sense of community; (2) collaborative planning and collegial relationships; (2) commonly shared clear goals and high expectations; and (4) order and discipline. As close examination reveals most, if not all of the 13 correlates could be subsumed under Edmonds' original list of 5 (see page 7).

> A school communi-cates... through the order and discipline it maintains

First impresions do count. Purkey and Smith placed particular stress on school climate. "A school communicates how serious and purposeful it is through the order and discipline it maintains in its buildings and classrooms," they said. Schools must create an atmosphere "conducive to the business at hand"—namely, teaching and learning.

A 1986 study written by John Roueche and George Baker of the University of Texas at Austin and published by the American Association of School Administrators furthered work on school climate correlates by spelling out some elements that make a school climate conducive to student success. According to Roueche and Baker, they include a sense of order, purpose, direction, and coherence; orderly classrooms; a student-centered focus; quality in both academic and co-curricular activities; a climate of optimism and high expectations; and organizational health.

Synthesis and Challenge

During the 1980s several researchers attempted to synthesize and integrate the wide range of effective schools research literature that had accumulated up to that point. Among them was Michael Cohen, a onetime colleague of Ronald Edmonds and current director of the National Governors' Association Task Force on Education. Cohen made three key points. First, he said, school effectiveness depends on effective classroom teaching. Second, effectiveness demands that the instructional program at the school site be carefully coordinated and managed. Third, effective schools engender a sense of shared values and culture among the students and staff.

Still another perspective on the effective schools correlates came in the form of a 1987 work by Lawrence C. Stedman, formerly a researcher with the Fairfax County, Virginia, public schools and now a professor at the State University of New York at Binghamton. Stedman felt that the correlates identified by Edmonds, Brookover, Lezotte and others "cannot be substantiated" because many schools in which the correlates we represent "still had extremely low levels of achievement." Stedman challenged the research that underlay Edmonds' correlates and instead came up with his own list of nine practices present in the effective schools he studied:

1. Skilled use and training of teachers.

2. Academically rich programs.

3. An accepting and supportive environment.

4. Teaching aimed at preventing academic problems.

5. Student responsibility for school affairs.

6. Ethnic and racial pluralism.

7. Parent participation.

8. Personal attention to students.

9. Shared governance with teachers and parents.

Brookover, in turn, charged that Stedman had based his criticisms on distorted and overgeneralized descriptions of the effective schools literature.

Many of Stedman's correlates (specifically, the first five on the list above) do not differ that widely from Edmonds or the Purkey and Smith correlates. The sixth—ethnic and racial pluralism—had not appeared on Edmonds' list although Edmonds and his colleagues had referred to it frequently. Edmonds in particular had denounced the practice of pull-out programs for disadvantaged children and had advocated school-wide efforts to address differing student needs and various student cultures.

The concept of shared governance, which Stedman viewed as an alternative to leadership that relied solely on one strong principle, was already being used in many school buildings, although not without some difficult struggles. School principals were often reluctant to give up decision-making authority, especially to parents, when it was the administrators who were ultimately held responsible for results.

Stedman's correlates pertaining to student responsibility and personal attention to students are noteworthy in that they helped lay the groundwork for subsequent work by Theodore Sizer, a Brown University researcher who, through his "Coalition for Essential Schools," has used the effective schools literature and other sources to create a blueprint for improving the quality of education in American high schools.

Critical Thinking and Effective Schools

In 1988, William W. Wayson and his associates at Ohio State University brought a new dimension to the effective schools discussion by integrating research in critical thinking instruction. According to Wayson and his colleagues, excellent schools can help students learn both basic skills and critical thinking skills by:

- Evaluating both the testing program and individual progress.

- Fostering conditions in which teachers can work together on bettering instruction, planning curriculum, solving problems, and improving the school.

- Coupling teacher evaluations with staff development programs to help teachers improve their skills.

- Maintaining extensive extracurricular programs for students.

- Involving parents.

What clearly set effective schools apart from less effective schools, said Wayson, was the presence of "cooperative working relationships among the staff."

Southwest Educational Development Lab: Parents and Schools

Although James Comer had been working on parental involvement since 1968, it was not until 1988 that the positive relationship between parental involvement and school effectiveness was clearly confirmed by a group of researchers working under the umbrella of the Southwest Educational Development Laboratory in Austin, Texas. Effective schools, said the laboratory researchers, "establish methods of communicating with parents, involve parents in the activities of the school, have parents serve as resources to extend the efforts of the school, include parents in the planning and decision-making, and depend on parents to provide good public relations for the school."

Installing Effective Schools Models

While the research base was still developing, local practitioners began installing effective schools approaches in their school buildings—mostly one school at a time. Some district-level administrators, such as Robert Sudlow, assistant superintendent for instruction at Spencerport, New York (a suburb of Rochester), started thinking about ways to implement the process across a whole school district. As Sudlow describes it, he and his superintendent, Joseph Clement, Jr., became intrigued by the fact that "numerous independent research studies conducted throughout the United States and England reported similar findings, something rare in education." What helped persuade Sudlow and Clement were the results of the models already functioning in other parts of New York, Connecticut, Wisconsin, California, and Michigan. With direct assistance from Edmonds and Lezotte, Spencerport began implementing a district-wide effective schools approach in 1982-83, one of the first districts to do so. On July 15, 1983, while working with Spencerport, Ronald Edmonds passed away.

Not long after Spencerport embarked on its effective schools odyssey, schools in Prince George's County, Maryland; Norfolk, Virginia; and Glendale, Arizona, among others, followed suit. Many large, urban districts, such as Milwaukee and New York City, also began using effective schools research findings to design and implement district-wide improvement programs.

Initial Fears

Implementation was by no means an easy process. As Lezotte wrote, "the effective schools research provided a vision of a more desirable place for schools to be, but gave little insight as to how best to make the journey to that place." In some cases, central offices or local school boards attempted to impose effective schools as a "top-down" reform, which clashed with the founding researchers' concept of the single school as the unit for reform. Other difficulties arose when principals concluded, incorrectly, that they were expected to create change single-handedly, or when teachers saw the new procedures as an affront to their teaching abilities or an administrative burden.

Recent statistics show that the process Edmonds helped forge is now operational in nearly 4,000 school districts in the United States and Canada, with more joining the ranks each year. The school reform movement of the past decade has helped power implementation of effective schools approaches. Seeking to respond to the public demand for comprehensive school improvement, many local school districts adopted effective schools initiatives as one viable response.

...principals concluded incorrectly, that they were expected to create change single-handedly...

The Larger Context

The most recent phase of implementation, while continuing to stress school-site reform, emphasizes the role of what Daniel Levine at the University of Missouri, Kansas City, and Lezotte call the "larger organizational contexts"—states, regions, and the whole nation—in supporting reforms in individual schools. Over the past few years, intermediate educational units, state departments of education, and the federal government have incorporated effective schools concepts into reform initiatives, with other proposals in the planning stages. Chapter 9 discusses these fresh developments in effective schools implementation in more detail.

As more schools wrestle with implementation, they are confronting challenges and problems not addressed by the existing research and models. The academic community has attempted to respond to this need by conducting additional research and pilot programs.

Currently, almost every major university in the United States and Canada is involved in effective schools research and its application in classrooms. Chapter 9 also examines in more detail some of these new research issues for effective schools.

What Is Needed To Implement the Process?

Local Flexibility

As the above description and history attempt to make clear, there is no single, pat definition of the effective schools process. The body of research lays out the basic correlates and the general responsibilities of the parties involved, but leaves most decisions about implementation to local practitioners. Because the target for improvement is the individual school building, Edmonds and other early researchers encouraged local school people to apply and adapt the process to suit their particular needs. When working with Connecticut schools, for example, Edmonds, Lezotte and their colleagues developed a questionnaire that schools could use to formulate school profiles and analyze local needs. As new empirical research and case studies yield more and different approaches to the effective schools process, the concept of local flexibility takes on even greater importance.

Correlation Is Not Causation

Analysts of the effective schools process have also taken care to point out, as Lezotte and Levine have, that "correlation is not causation" and that correlates "may not necessarily portray the variables that make some schools unusually effective, but instead may themselves be the product of unspecified processes, actions, and characteristics that lead both to higher achievement and to high scores . . . ." Research has also emphasized, as Stedman did, that each correlate "should be thought of as a set of highly interrelated practices, where efforts in one area will generally make it smoother in another."

No Quick Fix

If one lesson cuts across the research, it is Lezotte's caveat that "there is no quick fix." Researchers have stressed that implementing an effective schools process requires a three- to five-year commitment on the part of a school or a district.

Simply installing the process requires a substantial time commitment—two to three years, on average. During this period, administrators and teachers accustomed to traditional modes of instruction, such as lecturing, must be trained in other approaches to teaching and learning. The school's testing program must be aligned with the curriculum, and procedures must be put in place to separate test results by socioeconomic status, ethnicity, race, gender, and even attendance. In some cases, new tests must be designed, and new textbooks must be ordered.

One Step at a Time

Perhaps most significantly, it takes time to build support for and confidence in proposed changes among the school board and the community, whose support is essential to the outcome. Given all of these practical considerations, many districts have elected to implement the effective schools process by increments.

The effective schools process does not end with implementation. As Lezotte explained, "It isn't something you finish. It's a continuing—an endless—succession of incremental adjustments . . . What's done today needs to be evaluated and probably altered to meet the needs of tomorrow."

Nor can one expect instantaneous results. Professor Kent Peterson, director of the National Center for Effective Schools Research, told Norfolk, Virginia, educators that five to seven years is a realistic time to wait for results to appear. "This is real trench work," said Peterson. "Improvement should come at the rate of two or three percent a year in student achievement, but you have to keep slugging away at it."

The Importance of Planning

Experts have identified two factors as crucial to a school's success:

- The school must develop and state its mission; and

- The school must be willing to accept the effective schools process as a comprehensive program.

To ensure that these factors are built into the process from the beginning, researchers encourage each school, through a team planning approach involving administrators, faculty and parents, to develop and implement a long-range improvement plan, based on the correlates and elements of the effective schools knowledge base.

As Barbara Taylor of the NCES cautions, the opportunities to make lasting improvement diminish when the school improvement plan addresses only selected parts of the process. "Developing a school improvement plan on a piecemeal basis and focusing on only two or three of the correlates which define an effective school destroys the cohesiveness of the program and decreases the chance for significant and lasting improvement at the schools," says Taylor.

Conclusion

As this overview attempts to show, the effective schools concept is built on years of research and practical experience with implementation. Administrators who are interested in instituting the process in their schools must be prepared to make a comprehensive commitment over a period of years. The following chapters discuss each of the six major correlates in detail. (These include Edmonds' five correlates, plus parental and community involvement.)

SOURCES

Becker, Marc S.; Barry, Janet N.; "School Effectiveness at the Secondary Level: The Glendale Union Model." Edited by Barbara O. Tayor. *Case Studies in Effective Schools Research*. Madison, Wisconsin: National Center For Effective Schools Research, University of Wisconsin, 1990.

Brookover, Wilbur B. "Distortion and Overgeneralization Are No Substitutes for Sound Research." *Phi Delta Kappan* 69, 3. (November 1987): 225-227.

Brookover, Wilbur B.; Lezotte, Lawrence W. "Changes in School Characteristics Coincident with Changes in Student Achievement." Unpublished paper. East Lansing, Michigan: Michigan State University 181, 005.: p. 5.

Coleman, James S. *Equality of Educational Opportunity*. Washington, D.C.: U.S. Office of Education, National Center for Education Statistics, 1966.

Coleman, James S.; Hoffer, Thomas; and Kilgore, Sally. "High School Achievement: Public, Catholic, and Private Schools Compared." New York, N.Y.: *Basic Books*. (November 1982): 179-227. Also: Public and Private Schools. Washington, D.C.: U.S. Office of Education, National Center for Education Statistics, 1981.

Comer, James P. "Educating Poor Minority Children." *Scientific American* 259, 5 (November 1988): 42-48.

D'Amico, Joseph. "Each Effective School May Be One of a Kind" *Educational Leadership*, (1982): 61-62.

Edmonds, Ronald. "Effective Schools For The Urban Poor." *Educational Leadership* 37, 1 (October 1979): 16, 22, 23.

Edmonds, Ronald; Fredericksen, John. *Searching for Effective Schools: The Identification and Analysis of City Schools That Are Instructionally Effective for Poor Children*. Washington, D.C.: National Institute of Education 170, 396 (1979): 52.

Edmonds, Ronald . "A Discussion of the Literature and Issues Related to Effective Schooling." A paper prepared for the National Conference on Urban Education conducted by CEMREL, Inc., St. Louis, Mo.: (July 1978).

Edmonds, Ronald; Comer, James; Billingsley, Andrew; et al. "A Black Response to Christopher Jencks's Inequality and Certain Other Issues." *Cambridge, Mass.: Harvard Educational Review* 43 1 (February 1973): 45.

Good, Thomas L.; Brophy, Jere E. "School Effects." Ed., Wittock, Merlin C. *Handbook of Research on Teaching.* New York: Macmillan. (1986): 581-584.

Levine, Daniel U.; Lezotte, Lawrence W. *Unusually Effective Schools.* Madison, Wisc.: National Center for Effective Schools, 1990.

Lezotte, Lawrence W. *School Improvement Based on Effective Schools Research.* Okemos, Mich. (September 1989): 8-13

Lezotte, Lawrence W. "Base School Improvement on What We Know About Effective Schools." Washington, D.C.: *The American School Board Journal.* (August 1989): 18-20

Lezotte, Lawrence W.; Bancroft, Beverly A. "School Improvement Based on Effective Schools Research: A Promising Approach for Economically Disadvantaged and Minority Students." Albany, N.Y.: Effective Schools Consortia Network. New York State Department of Education. (April 1985).

Porter, Andrew C.; Brophy, Jere. "Synthesis of Research on Good Teaching: Insights from the Work of the Institute for Research on Teaching." *Educational Leadership* 45, 8 (1988): 74-85.

Purkey, Stewart; Smith, Marshall S. *Educational Policy and School Effectiveness.* Madison, Wisconsin: University of Wisconsin, School of Education, Wisconsin Center for Educational Research, 1984.

Purkey, Stewart, Smith, Marshall S. "Effective Schools: A Review." *The Elementary School Journal* (March 1983).

Roueche, John; Baker III, George. *Profiling Excellence in America's Schools.* Arlington, Virginia: The American Association of School Administrators, 1986.

Rutter, Michael, et al. *Fifteen Thousand Hours: Secondary Schools and Their Effects on Children.* Cambridge, Massachusetts: Harvard University Press, 1979.

Stedman, Lawrence C. "It's Time We Changed the Effective Schools Formula." Bloomington, Indiana: *Phi Delta Kappan* 69, 3 (November 1987): 215-224.

Steller, Arthur W. *Effective Schools Research:* Practice and Promise. Bloomington, Indiana: Phi Delta Kappa Educational Foundation, 1988.

Sudlow, Robert E. "Implementing Effective Schools Research in Spencerport, N.Y." Edited by Barbara O. Taylor. *Case Studies in Effective Schools Research.* Madison, Wisconsin: National Center for Effective Schools Research and Development, University of Wisconsin, 1990.

Wayson, William W. *Up from Excellence: The Impact of the Excellence Movement on Schools.* Bloomington, Indiana: Phi Delta Kappa Educational Foundation, 1988.

Weber, George. *"Inner-City Children Can Be Taught to Read: Four Successful Schools."* Washington, D.C.: The Council for Basic Education. Occasional papers number 18 (October 1971).

CHAPTER 2: STRONG LEADERSHIP

"Leadership is getting the job done through people."

—Scott Thompson, executive secretary, National Policy Board for Educational Administration

What Constitutes Strong Leadership?

Easy To Recognize, Hard To Define

Defining strong leadership—Edmonds' first correlate—is like trying to describe the taste of an orange. There are as many definitions as there are thinking people. For instance, when the American Association of School Administrators asked its members in a random survey to define strong instructional leadership, the organization received a host of responses, all of which reflected some important aspect.

Academics and practitioners have grappled with defining the elements of strong instructional leadership in ways that might help others acquire it. Warren Bennis and Burt Nanus, both professors at the University of Southern California specializing in leadership and management instruction, artfully summed up leadership as follows: "Leadership is like the Abominable Snowman, whose footprints are everywhere but who is nowhere to be seen."

Sharon E. Freden, assistant commissioner of education in Kansas and a respondent to the AASA survey, defined strong instructional leadership as "that which keeps instruction and the success of all children in school as the obvious first priority of the school." Thomas Fitzgerald, chief of the New York State Bureau of School Improvement, labeled it "the ability to influence the behavior of others to the point where that influence produces increased achievement for the students being served."

Others have approached the definition by attempting to delineate what it is that a strong leader does. For instance, Darrell K. Loosle, associate superintendent of the Idaho Department of Education, defined a strong leader as: "The principal who effectively communicates the mission of the school to parents, staff, and students and gives directions, emphasis,and support to the school's instructional program." Similarly, Marjorie Spaedy, director of the Missouri Department of Elementary and Secondary Education's leadership academy, pointed to strong instructional leadership as "the principal's pro-active role for providing direction, resources, and support to teachers and students for the improvement of teaching and learning in the school."

Motivation and vision. Penny Taylor, principal of Foothills Junior High School in Arcadia, California, interpreted a strong leader as a person who can easily "bring staff to a consensus on school vision, keep that vision in their sights, and motivate them to go for it. The leader must be willing to take risks — and defend staff members who do so for the improvement of the program. Results are this person's bottom line."

> The leader must be willing to take risks and defend staff members who do so

William Caudill, superintendent of Kings Local School District in suburban Cincinnati, described strong instructional leadership as, "Motivating staff to get the job done of educating students. Getting the 'education family' involved in a cooperative effort." Caudill knows first-hand what it takes to lead a school system and community; he earned his reputation as a mover and shaker when he instituted a year-round program for latchkey children in his Ohio district.

Leadership vs. Management

Some conspicuous themes run through many of the definitions. One important theme is that leadership and management are not necessarily the same. As Bennis and Nanus noted, "To manage means to bring about, to accomplish, to have charge or responsibility for, to conduct. Leading is influencing, guiding in direction, course, action, opinion. The distinction is crucial.

Managers are people who do things right, and leaders are people who do the right thing." Bennis and Nanus, who formulated many of their ideas by studying the leaders of large, successful companies, went on to explain that the difference between leadership and management "may be summarized as activities of vision and judgement—effectiveness—versus activities of mastering routines—efficiency."

"Leaders," they said, "do not spend their time on the 'how-tos,' the proverbial 'nuts and bolts,' but rather with the paradigms of action with 'doing the right thing.'"

Steven Bossert of the University of Utah's Department of Education Administration has a different take on the issue of management and leadership. Bossert likes the term "management of instruction" (as distinct from the old-style of school management) because it describes what the principal's primary role should be in an effective school.

Don't Throw Out the Old

This is not to say that traditional management skills are unnecessary. Effective principals at all grade levels use a variety of managerial skills every day to create an atmosphere in which good teaching and high achievement thrive. By efficiently "managing" their school's budget, staff, facilities, student services, and relationship with the community, they provide the necessary base for a strong school culture," said the authors of the U.S. Education Department's Principal Selection Guide.

A case in point: Bill Koller, the principal of Byng High School in Ada, Oklahoma, brought to bear his leadership and management skills when he undertook a major renovation of his building. Realizing that the dilapidated condition of the school was demoralizing students and inhibiting performance, Koller worked with pupils and faculty to acquire donated land and stockpile reasonably-priced building materials. Once the land and supplies were in place, Koller encouraged his vocational students and maintenance staff to handle the construction. The result, according to one visitor, is "a masterpiece of construction and architecture . . . that would be the envy of a large metropolitan school." Even more impressive than the exterior is the effect the renovation had on student and faculty attitudes: they no longer "think of themselves as poor; they think of themselves as resourceful," said Koller, as reported by Thomas Corcoran of the Philadelphia education laboratory, Research for Better Schools.

The Personal Dimension of Leadership

Many experts who have studied leadership point to personal qualities—creativity, high moral standards, the ability to inspire others, for example—as being among the chief determinants of a dynamic school leader. The U.S. Department of Education's *Principal Selection Guide* describes the personal qualities that make certain principals effective in this way: "They command attention, inspire respect, set high goals, and motivate teachers and students to meet them. They achieve these results not only because of what they do, but because of who they are."

Willingness To Take Risks

Another personal quality that is valued in the leadership arena is the willingness to take risks. As Leonard O. Pellicer, a professor in the Department of Educational Leadership and Policies at the University of South Carolina, says, "The more risks taken, the better the results." Pellicer's research emphasizes the link between student eagerness to learn, staff satisfaction, and the willingness of principals and their assistants to gamble on new ideas. "In cases where principals met resistance from a district," said Pellicer, "they sometimes exercised creative insubordination."

Notable Risk Takers

Frederick Zerlin. Frederick Zerlin, an elementary school principal in Miami, Florida, and *Tarja Geis*, one of his teachers, took advantage of the school-based management concept advocated by the Dade County Public Schools to create a new kind of elementary school—the Gilbert I. Porter School.

It is apparent at first glance that something exciting is happening at Porter: at the building's entryway, an electric marquee flashes messages about school activities to the community. Science is the school's specialty, and the staff work closely with the National Aeronautics and Space Administration. In keeping with the space theme, students are grouped by "galaxies" instead of grades, which means that an advanced 5-year-old and a less advanced 6-year-old learn together.

To determine individual student learning styles, entering children are tested. "Some students do best in the morning, some in the afternoon," Zerlin said. "Some like bright lights,

Continued

---

others don't. We'll use computers to figure out the best environment for each kid."

Joseph A. Spagnolo. Joseph A. Spagnola, superintendent for public instruction in Virginia, moved to the state level after encouraging his principals to take risks while he was superintendent of the Lynchburg, Virginia, public schools.

One visible achievement of Spagnolo's tenure at Lynchburg is the Pride Center, a school for dropouts and potential dropouts one observer called "the cutting edge of institutional stubbornness." The center, say school officials, is the main reason why Lynchburg's annual dropout rate fell from 7.3 percent to 3.1 percent in three years, under Spagnolo's leadership. "Successful efforts to combat dropouts," Spagnolo argues, "can't be all-encompassing things. They've got to be individual. One has to sit down with a youngster who says 'I'm leaving school' and really work with that youngster almost hand in glove, day by day."

That's exactly what the Pride staff does. One example: When an 18-year-old student who was also a teen mother fell behind in English to the point that it threatened to keep her from graduating, Pride administrators hired a teacher to help her cram for three days. In addition, James Strand, a social studies teacher, picked up the student at home and brought her to school. "He [Strand] actually held her infant baby while she took her exam, said Pride Center director Peyton Barbour. "I said to myself, 'Man, that's what it's all about.'"

Other Lynchburg principals also had positive words for the support they received from Spagnolo during his superintendency. "Spagnolo encourage[d] you to take risks if it [would] benefit the student," said Glass High School principal Roger E. Jones. "But if taking that risk [didn't] work, he [would] still be positive and encourage you to take that risk again."

Uniting the School Behind Common Goals

Another critical component of leadership is the ability "to help individuals with diverse beliefs and interests work toward common goals and objectives," according to Marvin Fairman, a professor at the University of Arkansas, Fayetteville; and Elizabeth Clark, assistant superintendent for instruction for the Hallsville, Texas, public schools. "The most effective leaders," said Fairman and Clark, "were those who were capable of uniting their faculties to accept common goals, thus building more cohesive organizations."

Synthesis of Leadership Research

James Sweeney, a professor at Iowa State University, attempted to synthesize research on specific leadership behaviors associated with effective schools and found that the following were mentioned most frequently: (1) emphasizing achievement; (2) setting instructional strategies; (3) providing an orderly school atmosphere; (4) frequently evaluating pupil progress; (5) coordinating instruction; and (6) supporting teachers.

The Role of the Principal

The Many Hats of the Principal

In the effective schools model, the school principal is a pivotal figure with diverse and important responsibilities. Mark Anderson, of the University of Oregon's School Study Council in Eugene, summed up the role of the principal in an effective school when he said, "The principalship is probably the most powerful force for improving school effectiveness and for achieving excellence in education . . . . The familiar adage, 'so goes the principal, so goes the school' is on the mark in characterizing the importance of a principal's leadership."

As the effective schools pioneers conceived of it, the principal is the leader who, working in cooperation with school improvement teams, can catalyze change in the way a school operates. To be successful, a principal in an effective school must assume many roles, including some that are not thought of as traditional for a building administrator. Steven Bossert attempted to spell out some of these roles. According to his research, effective principals:

- Are actively involved in setting instructional goals, developing performance standards for students, and expressing the belief that all students can achieve.

- Are more powerful than their colleagues, especially in the areas of curriculum and instruction. They also are seen as leaders in their districts and are effective in maintaining the support of parents and the community.

- Devote most of their time to the coordination and management of instruction and are highly skilled in instructional matters.

- Observe their teachers at work, discuss instructional problems, support teachers' efforts to improve their skills, and develop evaluation procedures that assess teacher and student performance.

- Clarify program and curricular objectives, and sustain schoolwide improvement efforts.

- Recognize the unique styles and needs of teachers, and help teachers achieve their own performance goals.

- Instill a sense of pride in the school among the teachers, students and parents.

Setting the Tone

Principals represent the organizational authority of the school, and as such set its tone. In the eyes of the public, the principal symbolizes what the school stands for, how it will operate, and what is important. Roland Barth of Harvard University has emphasized the need for the principal to set a moral tone for the school. "It's a question of moral leadership . . . You need to find somebody who can find the tall ground and stand on it," says Barth.

Creativity and courage also go into the mix. Bennis and Nanus make the point that leaders are not incrementalists. Rather, they are "people creating new ideas, new policies, new methodologies. They change the basic metabolism of their organizations." They are individuals who, in the words of French writer Albert Camus, are 'creating dangerously.'

A good principal can make the most of the authority and visibility inherent in the position by speaking often and clearly about the school's goals and objectives, and by directing the instructional program toward achieving those goals and objectives. According to the effective schools literature, principals must accept a shared responsibility for the school's attitudes, beliefs and expectations for students and, most of all, for the students' learning.

The Personal Qualities of a Strong School Leader

The effective principal:

- Elicits admiration because of integrity, knowledge, and skills which can achieve sparks of imagination and encourage imitation.

- Fosters a spirit of collegiality, cooperation and teamwork.

- Radiates an infectious enthusiasm for excellence.

- Prepares for victory even in defeat.

- Recognizes that schools require different leadership styles suited to specific situations and tailors actions to the needs of the faculty and students, the nature of the community and the school's history; for example, one school may have staffing problems, another disciplinary problems.

- Seeks creative solutions—even if it means taking risks.

Principal Selection Guide, U.S. Department of Education

Instructional Leadership

Perhaps the strongest message about leadership to emerge from the effective schools literature is the need for the building administrator to be an instructional leader. As Lezotte, one of the movement's founders noted, "When one runs into a quagmire of bureaucracy and lack of cooperation, a principal must ask: What is my central task? What is my absolute priority above all else as a school principal?" Lezotte has a ready answer to that question: "Teaching for learning."

Principals in More and Less Effective Schools

In a study of eight pairs of "more effective" and "less effective" Louisiana elementary schools, Robert Wimpelberg, a dean of the College of Education at New Orleans University and director of the New Orleans Principal Center, tried to learn more about what makes principals effective by engaging them in discussion about key effective schools concepts. He found some revealing differences:

On school mission. When asked to describe their school's mission, principals of less effective schools framed the mission in terms of the value systems of parents, rather than students. For example, principals of less effective schools spoke of their building's after-school program and health services. Principals of more effective schools, by contrast, described their school's mission in ways that were more child-oriented: "a child's refuge from a world of chaos"; "a positive climate without belittlement"; "a place where kids are taken care of with self-respect."

On monitoring progress. As regards Ronald Edmonds' fifth correlate, on progress toward instructional objectives (see page 7), principals in less effective schools said they kept abreast of students' progress through such means as checking report card grades, calling teachers into their office for periodic meetings, and, as one put it, having "the luxury" of a curriculum coordinator. Principals in more effective schools played much more active roles; they were common presences in their classrooms, observing instruction and sometimes leading lessons themselves.

On hiring and firing teachers. Principals in ineffective schools tended to follow bureaucratic guidelines in personnel matters, Wimpelberg found. In marked contrast, principals in effective schools had learned how to "play" the system to get the best teachers, even if it meant emphasizing the school's problems and "living in" the district's personnel office.

On the importance of basic skills. As regards Edmonds' fourth correlate, an emphasis on teaching basic skills, both groups of principals concurred that reading and math were of vital importance. They differed strongly, however, in their views about how challenging the instruction should be and how much emphasis basic skills should receive relative to other priorities. Principals in more effective schools viewed basic skills as "a link to higher order skills." As one said, "It's learning the basics and much much more." Principals in less effective schools seemed more willing to compromise their stated emphasis on basic skills. For example, some of the principals in the less effective group offered the disclaimer that basic skills instruction must be geared to the students' level; others insisted that additional priorities—"teaching self respect" or "classroom control" among them—deserved just as much emphasis.

On family background. According to Wimpelberg, principals in four of the sample's six less effective schools agreed that family background is the primary determinant of student achievement, while principals in four of the six more effective schools disagreed. One principal characterized the attitude of the less effective group when he said, "You try to put your values on these kids and they don't fit." Another principal of a socioeconomically mixed school complained that "non-affluent families simply lack concern, and we have a hard time overcoming that." In effective schools, Wimpelberg found, principals "accept differences among parents and attempt, in some cases, to influence them rather than complain about them." As one such principal said, "I work on parents' aspirations and discipline at home." Another summed up the attitude of the more effective group in this way: "Many pitiful kids have done well because of teachers and counselors; family expectations are important but not as important as the school's."

You try to put your values on these kids and they don't fit

A Highly Visible Presence

At 9 a.m. on a busy school day, Frank Steadman, principal of Northside Middle School in Norfolk, Virginia, proudly points to his desk, which is completely clear. Steadman gets his paperwork done by efficiently using clerical staff, freeing up time for him to be available and highly visible to both staff and students. When he walks the hallways, he greets students by name and speaks to them in a kindly way. Students passing by call his name, and when he answers, there is a mutual respect—a friendly admiration—reflected in their faces.

At Northside, there is no chaos between the 40-minute class periods. Classrooms are arranged by grade groupings so that students can walk to their next room, usually a few doors away. To foster camaraderie, the children are given a chance each year to name their groups after their favorite animals, such as the Bears and the Tigers.

Steadman exemplifies a quality that effective schools researchers have identified as a crucial component of leadership: high visibility. Visibility goes hand in hand with instructional leadership and support: a principal who sits in the office all day doing paperwork is not likely to know what goes on in the classrooms as well as one that is actively, visibly engaged.

Caring but Firm

The ability to set fair discipline standards also is a component of effective leadership. Deloris Hardiman, principal of Griffin

Elementary School in Cooper City, Florida, exemplifies the personal qualities needed. When Hardiman got word that "bus loads" of armed teenagers were approaching the high school grounds across the street from her school, she didn't waste a moment. She stood her ground when the cars and trucks the teenagers were driving had stopped. She directed the kids to line up, making enough noise to attract neighborhood attention; the kids complied. In a firm and deliberate manner she searched the teenagers one at a time. She had heard the kids talk of a "rumble" so she talked to them directly about death, pain, and the fact that she cared about them. "Later," she said, "parents called to protest that I had searched their child. I just told them that I was there to help their child because I cared about them." As a result of this incident, parents became her allies. Word spread about Hardiman's firm hand; there have been no more similar troubles at either Hardiman's school or the high school.

The Complexities of High School Leadership

At the high school level, effective leadership comes up against a different, and perhaps more complex, set of challenges. If frequent monitoring of teacher practices is a hallmark of good leadership, then high school principals face an impossible task, according to an 1986 study by Stewart Purkey, then at Lawrence University, and Robert Rutter, then with the University of Wisconsin at Madison. As these researchers pointed out, one cannot improve high school leadership simply by mandating more supervision, because a variety of factors impinge on the time available for supervision. For example, noted Purkey and Rutter:

- "In a building with 100 teachers, close to 400 hours, or 10 weeks, would be consumed by supervision (this assumes two hours per person, per session, a pre-conference observation of the entire class period, and a follow-up conference), a rather expensive outlay of resources;

- "All teachers may not need the same amount of supervision, all may not welcome increased amounts of it"; moreover, classroom test scores "may obscure . . . situationally-based variations" in teacher effectiveness;

- "Test scores . . . reveal nothing about the quality of supervision, which is likely to be of more importance than its frequency."

University of South Carolina professor Leonard Pellicer, who studied 78 high schools that ranked at or above average in terms of student achievement, agrees that the job of high school principal has become increasingly complex and now demands an extraordinary type of person. "When we started out with education in America, we basically brought kids to school and taught them reading, writing and arithmetic," said Pellicer. "Now we transport them, we feed them, we give them career counseling, personal counseling. Everything is so much more complicated and it takes a different kind of person to maintain a grasp of what's going on."

In his report, entitled "High School Leaders and Their Schools," Pellicer found that principals cope with these demands by sharing responsibility. According to Pellicer, instructional leadership was most commonly exercised by "department chairpersons, with the support of a school administrative team and the assistance of district supervisors." The focus of the leadership, according to Pellicer, was "planned change in the school's instructional program through influencing and directing behaviors [of students and teachers]."

Delegating and Sharing Leadership

As Pellicer's research suggests, effective principals carry out their legion responsibilities by knowing when and to whom to delegate. Many researchers have noted that elementary and middle or junior high school administrators do not delegate enough. "Choosing the right delegates is in itself a form of leadership," says Joan Shoemaker of the Connecticut Department of Education and a fellow of the National Center for Effective Schools Research. "Keep an eye on what and to whom you delegate, but do not try to do everything by yourself," she advises.

More recently, researchers have emphasized that it is a mistake for school-site administrators to view the effective schools leadership correlate as a mandate to "go it alone." Increasingly, researchers and practitioners are emphasizing the importance of a collegial, collaborative process that involves all the adults in the school, especially the teachers. In this organizational structure, the principal becomes, as Lezotte has noted, a "leader of leaders . . . [a] coach, partner and cheerleader."

The Role of the Superintendent

"It would be a serious, if not fatal mistake to ignore the essential roles of superintendents and school boards," said *The Role of the Principal in Effective Schools*, an American Association of School Administrators publication. "For if the principal embodies the potential for creating the conditions that breed good schools, it is the superintendent directly and the school board indirectly who either deter or enable principals to fulfill their potential." Continued the report: "It is obvious that superintendents and the school boards, through the policies and the priorities they set and the resources allocated to back up those policies, exert an enormous influence on principals."

Superintendents agree that nurturing principals is a key role, especially when a school is striving to become an effective school. "The care and feeding of principals is the single most important thing a superintendent can do," said Gordon L. McAndrew, former superintendent of the Richland County School District in Columbia, South Carolina.

Just what is the best way for superintendents to accomplish this? Most principals feel that regular communication between superintendent and principals is imperative, as is being supportive and giving verbal recognition. In addition, say principals, the superintendent might work with them on setting school improvement goals. (This is not to suggest that principals want the superintendent to interfere in their decision-making.) Principals have also asked that superintendents give them more authority.

What Do Administrators Need?

Once the leadership roles in effective schools are made clear, the question arises: Are administrators prepared to fill these roles? In the AASA survey, respondents were generally optimistic about the capabilities of those currently leading our nation's schools. Fifty-one percent of the 140 respondents ranked strong leadership as their number one priority, and 56 percent thought it was present in their schools to "a great extent" or "a very great extent."

The findings of Gary D. Gottfredson, with the Johns Hopkins University Center for Research on Elementary and Middle Schools, indicate at least some correspondence between how principals view their jobs and what an effective schools model demands of them. According to Gottfredson, principals see staff direction, teacher observation, feedback on teacher performance, and planning for school improvement as key dimensions of their work.

The Need for Professional Development

Despite these relatively positive assessments, there is a widespread feeling, both inside and outside the education profession, that a strong need exists for education leadership training and revised certification on the state and local levels. The report of the National Governors' Association Task Force on Education recommended that "states, working with education, business, and community leaders, must design a system for licensure based on what school administrators need in order to lead, manage and succeed in a restructured education system." The Task Force went on to recommend that administrators "make professional development a vital part of the job." Effective schools experts further recommend that local school boards accept more responsibility for inservice administrator training, particularly new training models that emphasize leadership as an essential competency.

Top 5 Qualities of Leadership

Respondents to the AASA survey for this book identified the following as the qualities and focuses most valued in school leaders:

	% Ranking it #1*
1. Strong instructional leadership	51
2. High expectations for students	24
3. A safe, orderly, and disciplined school climate	12
4. District-level support for school improvement	8
5. Staff concensus on specific instructional goals	7

Numbers do not add up to 100 because of multiple responses.

Sources

Kukeris, Misty. *Time On Task.* Arlington, Va.: American Association of School Administrators, 1982.

Selecting a Superintendent. Arlington, Va.: A joint publication of American Association of School Administrators and the National School Boards Association, 1979.

Amundsen, Kristen. *Challenges for School Leaders.* Arlington, Va: The American Association of School Administrators, 1988.

"The Good Principal: A Tradition Breaker." *The New York Times,* February 21, 1990.

Bagin, Don; Ferguson, Donald; Marx, Gary. *Public Relations for Administrators.* Arlington, Va.: The American Association of School Administrators, 1985.

Barth, Roland, S. "The Principalship," *Education Leadership* 42, 6 (March 1985): 92-94.

Bennis, Warren; Nanus, Burt. *Leaders: The Strategies for Taking Charge.* New York: Harper & Row, 1985.

Bossert, Steven; Dwyer; David; Lee, Ginny . "The Instructional Management Role of The Principal." *Educational Administration Quarterly* 18, 3 (Summer 1982): 34-64

Bossert, Steven. "Reaching for Excellence." Ed. Regina M.J. Kyle. *An Effective Schools Sourcebook.* Washington: U.S. Department of Education, Office of Educational Research and Improvement (OERI), 1986.

Boyer, Thomas. "City Takes Chances on 'At-Risk' Students, Lynchburg Educator is Credited." Norfolk, Virginia: *The Virginian-Pilot,* June 17, 1990.

Corcoran, Thomas B; and Wilson, Bruce L. "The Search for Successful Secondary Schools." Philadelphia, Pennsylvania: *Research for Better Schools,* (1986): 61.

Corcoran, Thomas B. "Effective Secondary Schools." Edited by Regina Kyle M.J. *An Effective Schools Sourcebook.* Washington: OERI. (1986): 55-97.

Davis, Gary A.; Thomas, Margaret A. *Effective Schools and Effective Teachers.* New York: Allyn and Bacon, 1989.

Smith, Stuart C.; and Piele, Philip K., eds. *School Leadership* (Second Edition). Portland, Oregon: ERIC Clearinghouse on Educational Management (1989): 2,4,5, 9-27.

Fiske, Edward B. "Lessons." *The New York Times,* April 18, 1990.

Gottfredson, Gary D. *An Analytical Description of the School Principal's Job.* Baltimore, Maryland: Center For Research On Elementary & Middle Schools, The Johns Hopkins University. Report No. 13. (May 1987): 126.

Levine, Daniel U.; Lezotte, Lawrence W. *Unusually Effective Schools.* Madison, Wisconsin: National Center for Effective Schools, 1990.

Lezotte, Lawrence W. *Correlates of Effective Schools: The First and Second Generations.* (1989): 3-4.

Lezotte, Lawrence W. *Strategic Assumptions of the Effective Schools Process.* Okemos, Michigan. (1989): 9.

Lezotte, Lawrence W. *School Learning Climate and Student Achievement.* East Lansing, Michigan: Center for Urban Affairs, Michigan State University. (1983): 83-92, 113-131.

McCurdy, Jack. *The Role of the Principal in Effective Schools: Problems & Solutions.* Arlington, Virginia: American Association of School Administrators, 1983.

National Governors' Association, Task Force on Education. *Strategies For Achieving The National Education Goals.* Washington, D.C., (June 1990): 39.

National School Boards Association. *A Blueprint for Educational Excellence. A School Board Member's Guide.* Washington, D.C., (1984): 52-55.

Pellicer, Leonard O.; Anderson, Lorin; Keefe, James W.; Kelly, Edgar A.; and McCleary, Lloyd E. *High School Leaders and Their Schools.* Reston, Va.: National Association of Secondary School Principals, 2 (1990): 58, 60-62.

Purkey, Stewart C; and Rutter, Robert A. *High School Teaching: Teacher Practices and Beliefs in Urban and Suburban Public Schools.* Madison, Wisc.: National Center on Effective Secondary Schools, School of Education, University of Wisconsin, 1986.

Rouche, John E.; and Baker, George. *Profiling Excellence in America's Schools.* Arlington, Va.: American Association of Schools Administrators, 1989, pp. 15, 16, 17.

Russell, James S.; Mazzarella, Jo Ann; White, Thomas; and Maurer, Steven. *Linking the Behaviors of Secondary School Principals to School Effectiveness.* Portland, Oregon: Center for Educational Policy, University of Oregon, 1985.

Sergiovanni, Thomas J. *The Principalship: A Reflective Practice Perspective.* New York: Allyn and Bacon, 1987.

Sweeney, James. "Research Synthesis on Effective School Leadership." *Educational Leadership.* (February 1982): 350.

U.S. Department of Education. *Good Secondary Schools: What Makes Them Tick?* Washington, D.C.: OERI. (1986): 3.

U.S. Department of Education. *Principal Selection Guide.* Washington: OERI, 1987, pp. 3, 4, 9, 10.

Wimpelberg, Robert K. "Managerial Images and School Effectiveness." Ann Arbor, Michigan: Administrator's Notebook. The Midwest Administration Center, The University of Chicago, 32, 4, 1987.

CHAPTER 3: A SAFE AND ORDERLY SCHOOL CLIMATE

"When a school has a "winning climate," people feel proud, connected, committed. They support, help, and care for each other. When the climate is right, there is a certain joy in coming to school, either to teach or to learn."

— James Sweeney

The Importance of School Climate

Ronald Edmonds defined a positive school climate as "the extent to which the whole environment supports the primary purpose of the enterprise"—in other words, an environment in which teachers can teach and students can learn. The characteristics that make up a positive environment are many: the school ought to be safe, orderly, clean, quiet, pleasant, unoppressive, and in good repair. Any distraction that interferes with classroom learning should be minimized and, to the extent possible, eliminated.

Some researchers further define climate to include human values, such as the ethos espoused by the school; the degree of cooperation among administration, faculty, and students; and the system of management.

As research has demonstrated, a positive environment is more dream than reality in many cases. In all too many of the schools Edmonds visited, he found an abundance of disruptions: announcements on the public address system, disorder in the halls, a stream of visitors interrupting the learning process.

Factors that Create a Positive Climate

Schools that find their climate wanting can take steps to improve it, as Jim Sweeny has noted in his list of 10 steps to a winning school climate:

1. A supportive, stimulating environment
2. Student-centered
3. Positive expectations
4. Feedback
5. Rewards
6. A sense of family
7. Closeness to parents and community
8. Communication
9. Achievement
10. Trust

A Clear Disciplinary Policy

In mentioning safety, Edmonds emphasized the need for a consistent disciplinary policy as a major contributor to climate. Adults in the school, said Edmonds, are responsible for managing the students; to accomplish this, they must get together, agree on the rules that govern the school, and enforce those rules all the time.

A clear and consistent disciplinary policy (and attendance policy) can have a noticeable impact on school climate, according to a five-year, ongoing study aimed at improving middle school discipline conducted by the Johns Hopkins Center for Research on Elementary and Middle Schools. When the six urban schools in the study revised their discipline policies to clarify the rules, spell out the consequences of breaking the rules, and coordinate the schoolwide policy with individual classroom teachers, the result was a dramatic drop in disciplinary problems after three years.

A key component of the new policies in these six schools has been a shift in the focus of adult-student relationships, from a system based mostly on punishment to one based primarily on rewards. Another critical component is teacher training in classroom organization and management; teachers are taught to clearly communicate rules, monitor student behavior, and provide follow-up for students who break the rules. Effective instructional practices and the use of specific methods to increase desirable behaviors for individuals and entire classes are other components of the Center's study.

Each school in the study has also set up a computerized system that tracks incidents of good and bad behavior, generates letters to parents about their children's behavior, and produces reports used to manage school discipline.

An AASA Critical Issues Report, *Student Discipline*, lists several approaches for improvement, including teaching by example, assertive discipline, and reality therapy.

Small things count. Even small gestures can make a difference in student behavior. Thomas McCullough, principal of Kishwaukee Elementary School in Rockford, Illinois, tells the story of a teacher's attempt to boost attendance and reduce tardiness. "[O]ne of my second grade teachers decided to greet her students at the door every day with a cheery 'good morning' and give each student a sticker on the back of his or her hand as each came in," said McCullough. "This small gesture did more to inspire children to come to school on time than anything else."

Physical Condition of the School

One way to head off discipline problems before they surface is to keep the school in shipshape physical condition at all times. A school in disrepair may send a subconscious message of neglect that may be picked up by teachers, children, parents, and the community. As Edmonds said, "[I]t matters whether or not you repair a broken window. It has less to do with the window and more to do with the fact that if it stays broken, you'll see it for a long time, and you'll conclude that nobody cares about the school."

School administrators who responded to the AASA survey countered that keeping up the physical condition of a school is often an expensive proposition, and that the funds are often not available to replace old facilities, provide space for increased enrollments, or make needed repairs. One way to improve the physical condition of the school without spending a great deal of money, however, is to enlist the aid of students. They can help paint, clean up and beautify the school grounds, for example. An added benefit is that students who feel they've contributed to improved surroundings are less likely to vandalise or deface their own "work."

Pro-Social Skills Training

Noelle Branch, principal of Loma Linda Elementary School in Colorado's St. Vrain Valley School District, a mountain community north of Denver, realized she had a serious disciplinary problem when large numbers of students in grades K-3 were being referred to her office for disrupting class.

Pinpoint the problem. Loma Linda participates in the Colorado Onward to Excellence program, a variation of the effective schools model that calls for leadership teams in each school. The Loma Linda team established as its primary goal the improvement of discipline. Staff members followed up by identifying specific disciplinary problems.

After reviewing the approaches for addressing these problems, staff members decided that the answer lay with a "pro-social" skills training program called Skillstreaming. Originally developed for use with special education students, Skillstreaming is based on the premise that behavioral problems are the result of skill deficits and that to remediate behavioral problems, students must learn the skills of self-management and getting along with others.

Skill-of-the-month. In the Loma Linda program, each of the school's priority skill areas—classroom skills such as listening, asking questions, and seeking clarifications, or friendship skills such joining in and being honest—becomes a schoolwide focus for a month. Faculty volunteers lead the monthly training efforts, using their own teaching approach. Teachers use role playing, poster contests, or outside speakers, to give a few examples, to highlight the skill of the month. School staff, including classified staff, give out buttons to students they see practicing the skill of the month. A student awards assembly is also held each month to reinforce positive behavior.

Principal Branch is enthusiastic about this program. "We have to give kids tools for interacting with others successfully and opportunities to use those tools," she said. Statistics corroborate that the program is reaping results. In the year before the program's onset, 77 first-graders were referred to the principal's office for disciplinary action. In a recent year, fewer than five first-graders were referred.

The Personality of the School

Any teacher, parent, student or administrator who has spent time in one school and moves to another soon recognizes that each school has its own personality, or ethos, that becomes apparent soon after entering its doors. This personality is the sum of many parts, not the least of which are the values espoused, exemplified, and rewarded (which may not always be the same) by the principal, teachers, other staff, and even parents.

Poverty can alienate. Elementary schools in socioeconomically disadvantaged areas face unique challenges trying to build a positive school personality amid an environment of negative social influences and parent alienation from the schools. When alienation between home and school exists, according to James Comer, it is "difficult to nurture a bond between child and teacher that can support development and learning," and this, in turn, can have a strong effect on school climate. The answer, says Comer, is mutual respect: "[I]f you create a climate which enables people to relate to each other with respect, and support each other, then you can better manage the stresses that are normal in school systems . . . you can create a climate where you can develop a commitment to get along and to do the best possible job . . . ."

> When alienation between home and school exists, it is difficult to nurture a bond between child and teacher

Additional administrative and teacher training aimed at fostering sensitivity and awareness may be necessary for this to happen. Comer tells the story of a first-grade teacher in an inner-city school who, on the first day of school, explained the classroom rules. "When she finished," said Comer, "a six-year-old raised his hand and said, 'Teacher, my mama said I don't have to do anything you say.' Fortunately this teacher understood the underlying problem, but most teachers would have reacted angrily, whereupon any chance of gaining parental cooperation would have quickly evaporated."

How Comer and other researchers, teachers, and administrators are working to involve parents in schools is discussed further in Chapter 7.

A Spirit of Cooperation

Research has also stressed the importance of collegiality in building an effective school climate. Edmonds believed that although it is not always necessary for school staff to get along, it is always their "obligation to cooperate." Said Edmonds: "I talk about the obligation to have a shared set of professional behaviors to which it is absolutely essential that all subscribe."

James Comer makes the related point that where conflicts among staff are unavoidable, these disagreements should not be voiced openly among students because it could carry over to the children's behavior. "If the children see two teachers yelling at each other, i.e., Mr. Jones yelling at Ms. Smith," said Comer, "then the kids will do the same thing . . . yell at Ms. Smith."

Student/Faculty Relations

Clarkston Junior High School in Clarkston, Michigan, has sought to improve the school climate by emphasizing student self-image and student relationships with faculty and administrators. According to Vincent F. Licata, an assistant principal, the school has undertaken several new efforts, including the development of "a school mission that emphasizes that every student will receive at least one success experience a year"; a teacher advisor program that matches every student with one special adult in the school; and a regular schedule of "play nights," in which faculty and students play sports together.

Systematic Management a Must

Edmonds also stressed the need for a systematic management process in every school, which encompasses academic policies, disciplinary policies, assessment and monitoring, and, in the most highly developed cases, personnel management and resource allocation. According to Edmonds, poor management is the root of a host of problems in ineffective schools. "If you don't have a procedure for dealing with behavior problems in some kind of systematic way in your schools, that is poor management," explained Edmonds. "If you don't have a procedure for academic goals for the year; and if you don't have a strategy for doing that on a yearly basis, a way of monitoring that, a time set up to look at your findings and modify your program, that is poor management. And most schools, or many schools don't have that. Even lots of suburban schools don't have that kind of systematic management process."

Tearing Down To Build Up

When Al Doan, principal of the Lynch Wood Elementary School in Portland, Oregon, became concerned about the inadequate reading performance of 40 percent of his pupils, he called in his "leadership team," consisting of himself, a central office representative, and key teachers. Together they decided on an approach that called for major changes in the use of staff, teacher scheduling, and even the physical arrangement of the building.

A learning center. To start, they had a large doorway cut between the Chapter 1 and special education resource rooms and named the larger space the "learning center." Now, during first-and second-grade reading periods, all regular classroom, special education, and Chapter 1 teachers and aides engage in 45 minutes of direct reading instruction, with no interruptions permitted. Three regular classroom teachers work with groups of 15 students each, while the Chapter 1 and special education teachers and aides work with small groups of four to eight students in different sections of the learning center. Wall charts of daily performance provide children with symbolic reinforcement of their learning successes. Sometimes the regular classes change places with the learning center groups in order to ensure there is no stigma associated with learning center classes.

Creative compliance. Doan and his staff have found ways to organize staffing creatively and still comply with federal Chapter 1 and handicapped program guidelines. For one thing, says Doan, "although Chapter 1 guidelines specify that students must be performing below grade level to be eligible for services, the individual school is at liberty to determine what grade level is, based upon internal reviews." Doan also points out that federal guidelines allow other kinds of flexibility. For example, non-special education students can receive special education services if they are under a monitoring system, and special education students can receive Chapter 1 services if so specified in their Individualized Education Plans. So far, the Lynch Wood arrangements have passed muster with federal program monitors.

School-Site Management

A good systematic management approach can form the foundation for the sort of school-site management prescribed by effective schools researchers and others. Comer, for example, believes that given the complexity of schools today, no school can be effectively run by just one principal. The answer, many feel, lies with leadership teams: a decision-making body consisting of administrators, faculty, other staff, parents, and even students at the senior high level.

As they have been implemented in many schools, leadership teams can be a vehicle for facilitating change and building school-wide and community-wide support, even when there is a strong principal. For example, in the school districts of Colorado, a state that participates in the Onward to Excellence school improvement process, building-level leadership teams compile profiles of school performance, and school staff select improvement goals based on those profiles. Staff then review relevant research, develop prescriptions and plans for reaching the identified goals, implement those plans, monitor operations, and periodically review and renew school improvement efforts.

Creating Positive Behaviors

The newest wave of effective schools research urges schools to move beyond reducing undesirable behavior toward building desirable behaviors, such as cooperative learning and respect for cultural diversity and democratic values. Some schools have already embarked on this path and have overcome the challenges presented by these efforts—more time and commitment from staff and students, for example; these schools can serve as beacons for others that are interested in fostering a truly collaborative climate.

SOURCES

Brodinsky, Ben. *Student Discipline: Problems and Solutions.* Arlington, Va., The American Association of School Administrators, 1980.

Comer, James P. "Educating Poor Minority Children." *Scientific American* 259, 5 (November 1988): 42-48.

Coppedge, Floyd L.; Exendine, Lois. "Improving School Climate by Expanding the Dimensions of Reinforcement." Reston, Va.: The National Association of Secondary School Principals *Bulletin 71,* 479 (March 1987): *ERIC Journal Index* 352, 259.

Cotton, Kathleen. "Creative Staffing Arrangements: Lynch Wood Elementary School." *School Improvement Research Series.* Portland, Ore.: Northwest Regional Education Laboratory, (January 1989): 2,3,4.

Cotton, Kathleen. "Improving Student Attitude and Behavior: Loma Linda Elementary School." *School Improvement Research Series.* Portland, Ore.: Northwest Regional Educational Laboratory, (1989): 2.

Fairman, Marvin; Clark, Elizabeth. "Moving Toward Excellence: A Model To Increase Student Productivity." Reston, Va.: National Association of Secondary Schools Principals *Bulletin* (January 1985): 6-11.

Gottfredson, Denise G.; Gottfredson, Gary D.; and Karweit, Nancy. *"Reducing Disorderly Behavior in Middle Schools."* Baltimore, Maryland: The Johns Hopkins University Center for Research on Elementary and Middle Schools. (April 1989): Report 37.

Hopkins, Willard; Crain, Kay. "School Climate: The Key to an Effective School." Paper presented at the annual meeting of the National Association of Secondary School Principals, New Orleans, La., January 1985.

Hoyle, John R.; English, Fenwick W.; Steffy, Betty E. *Skills for Successful School Leaders.* Arlington, Va.: American Association of School Administrators, 1985.

Lezotte, Lawrence W. *Correlates of Effective Schools: The First and Second Generations,* 1989, pp. 3-4.

Licata, Vincent F. "Creating a Positive School Climate at the Junior High Level." Paper presented at the annual meeting of the Michigan Association of Middle School Educators, Birmingham, Mich., March 1987.

Lindelow, John; Mazzarella, Jo Ann, et al. Eds. Smith, Stuart C.; and Piele, Philip K. *School Leadership, 2nd Edition.* Oregon: College of Education, University of Oregon, ERIC Clearinghouse on Educational Management. (1989): 168-188.

National Center for Effective Schools Research. *A Conversation Between James Comer and Ronald Edmonds.* Dubuque, Iowa: Kendall/Hunt Publishing Co., 1989.

Roueche, John E., Baker, George A. III. *Profiling Excellence In America's Schools.* Arlington, Va: The American Association of School Administrators, 1989.

Strong, Penny, Schlorf, Bette Wilson. *Urban Education; Urban and Ethnic Education Projects.* Springfield, Ill.: Illinois State Board of Education, 1989.

CHAPTER 4: HIGH EXPECTATIONS FOR STUDENT LEARNING

"People typically behave in ways consistent with the expectations others have for them or those they have for themselves."

— Arthur W. Steller, Superintendent,
Oklahoma City Public Schools

Expectations Influence Outcomes

Children differ dramatically. Some come to school already knowing how to read, while others can barely do so after years of trying. Some quickly pick up whatever new material is presented; others struggle to master rudimentary skills. But effective schools advocates do not accept these differences as excuses for inferior school performance. At the heart of the effective schools movement is this governing precept: all children can learn, at least to the minimum mastery level. Achieving this goal is the responsibility of the school and its staff. When teachers believe—or at least run their classrooms as though they believe—that all children can learn, then the likelihood that children will learn is enhanced.

The role of expectations in student learning is a frequently discussed topic in the effective schools literature. Research on expectations has firmly established that students for whom teachers have low expectations receive less academic work, less rigorous work, and are judged against lower standards. Teacher expectations about poor and minority children were of particular concern to the founders of the effective schools movement. "There are some teachers and administrators who don't believe these kids can learn," said James Comer. "There are parents who resent these attitudes but feel at the mercy of those teachers and administrators who feel their kids can't learn. There is a system that is resistant to change ." Comer felt it was incumbent on schools to "address that group of kids. That's what effective schools are all about."

Administrator Views on High Expectations

If the survey AASA conducted for this publication is any indication, administrators have a wide range of opinions about the significance of high expectations and the acceptance of high expectations in their school systems. Although the majority of school administrators believe that high expectations for students should be a top priority, a considerably lower proportion believe that this actually occurs in their schools, according to the AASA survey.

When asked to rank high expectations for student achievement from a list of priorities for their schools, 63 percent of the survey's 146 respondents ranked it among their top three priorities, and 24 percent ranked it first. When the same administrators were

---

A Bedrock Belief: Expectations Too Low for Too Long

The National Governors' Association Education Task Force addressed the issue of high expectations in a 1990 report on implementing the national goals for education developed by the president and the governors. "Restructuring efforts must rest on a bedrock belief that all students can learn at high levels. Students with special needs, or from poor and minority backgrounds, have long suffered from the unambitious expectations set for them," said the task force, directed by Michael Cohen. "Performance expectations for all students have been too low for too long. This is reflected in an unchallenging curriculum and in testing programs that highlight a narrow range of mostly low-level skills. Progress has more to do with accumulating seat time and course credits than with demonstrating required competencies."

"Educating America: State Strategies for Achieving the National Educational Goals."

asked to what extent having high expectations was *actually* a priority in their schools, 32 percent said, "to a moderate extent," and only 15 percent said, "to a very great extent."

The written comments on the survey were even more telling about the views practitioners held on high expectations. At one end of the spectrum were those who felt that it was unrealistic to presume that socioeconomic background does not affect learning. As one superintendent in rural Tennessee said, "Expectations are too high for all students." Despite his opinion, he noted, attitudes of high expectations for all children were present in his district "to a considerable extent." About 40 percent of the schools in his district, which serves over 4,000 students, voluntarily participate in the effective schools process, and these schools report "high learning expectations for all students—including at-risk, disadvantaged and 'hostile' children."

Great Expectations

A different opinion was exemplified by H. Dale Winger, superintendent of the Frazier School District in rural Perryopolis, Pennsylvania. Winger reported that in the past five years, the most important innovation behind improved effectiveness in his schools was, "establishing the principle that all children can learn and setting high expectancy levels."

In at least some cases, administrators gave high ranking to expectations as a priority, yet felt they currently were being neglected. For example, Irene Bandy, Ohio assistant superintendent of schools, said she ranked high expectations for student achievement as a third priority because the commitment to high expectations among Ohio teachers was already present to a considerable extent. Sharon Freden, assistant commissioner for the Kansas State Department of Education and a survey respondent, expressed concern that "high expectations for all students are not necessarily held by all." Although Freden ranked high expectations as the first priority for her state, she reported that it was present in Kansas schools "to a moderate extent."

A Subtle Problem

In many schools, the existence of low expectations can be a subtle or even hidden problem. As James Comer has noted, when teachers are asked the question, "Do you have high expectations?" almost all will respond, yes; but when asked, "Do you think that all the teachers in the school have high expectations?" most will say, no.

Edmonds made the point on several occasions that "prospective teachers ought to be taught that there are now alternative interpretations of the origin of achievement"; specifically, the interpretation that it is a school's response to a child's background of disadvantage—and not the background itself—that inhibits learning. As Edmonds said, "Accepting one or the other of those interpretations has profound implications for a teacher's choice of teaching strategies."

Thorny Attitudes About Student Ability

In 1982, the Glendale Union High School District in suburban Phoenix, Arizona, already had a reputation for excellence. Its student body was from mostly middle- to upper-income families, and a number of innovative programs existed in the schools. Yet, for the relatively small proportion of poor and disadvantaged children in the district, teacher attitudes were a problem. Many teachers held the view, albeit subtle, that less affluent kids could not learn as well as more affluent children, said Marc Becker, the district's research specialist. The situation came to a head over the issue of reporting test results. According to Becker, many administrators and faculty throughout the district wanted differences in student background to be included in the district's summary of student achievement. "Some teachers," said Becker, "claimed that students from poor families could not be expected to learn as much as their more affluent peers." Others disagreed.

"First you need to recognize this problem," explained Becker. When this recognition occurred, in school year 1982-83, the district, with the support of the superintendent, invited effective schools researchers to come in and help. Glendale instituted an approach to testing that aimed for well-distributed scores throughout the student population without regard for socioeconomic or family background status. That meant an end to teaching practices that sorted and selected students.

Fostering High Expectations

The Problem of Resistance

The past two decades of research on school effectiveness and child development have yielded ample evidence that expectations can indeed be changed. Part of the process is getting teachers and administrators to overcome their resistance to change and understand the possibilities and rewards created by high expectations for pupils.

A Feeling of Hopelessness

"A resistance is there when you ask teachers and principals to do more work," said Comer. "They believe that you are simply asking them to go along with another one of those liberal dreams, and it is not going to work better than any other liberal dream that they've been asked to try . . . The question is how to bring about change without anybody's feelings being threatened—without people feeling that nothing is going to do any good in the long run.

"Our approach," continued Comer, "is to get in and make change occur, so that the change in itself breaks the resistance, rather than telling people what they must know so that these kids can learn." He warned that "if you take the other approach and say this is the way it is; here is what you must do to make change happen; you suggest to teachers that they are not doing what they should be doing. That only adds to their resistance."

The results of the AASA survey suggest that in many cases, resistance to change may be less a function of stubbornness and more a reaction to a host of real-life problems that hamstring the best intentions of school people. Responding administrators pointed to such factors as limited resources for teacher training, mandated programs, and special services for at-risk children; and a lack of community support as inhibiting their ability to make changes.

Need for Training

Effective schools experts concur that teacher training and retraining is a must if expectations are to be changed. Edmonds maintained that the desire to change was there, if the right training opportunities were offered. When he and his collaborator Lawrence Lezotte offered training opportunities for elementary schools, 100 percent of the superintendents from 21 of the largest school districts in Michigan accepted the invitation to send five staff members. "We answered the issue of educability of the kids by telling them [the staff people in training] we would not address the issue of attitude," Edmonds said. "We would merely say, we know how to teach the attainable professional behaviors that will predictably produce mastery—minimum mastery, that is...

"We tell them: We are not going to ask you to do anything that we can't teach you how to do, if you ask us," added Edmonds. "I think that we allay anxiety because we don't ask people to do things we can't teach them how to do. Apparently they believe in us." Once they accepted the premise that "change" was necessary, said Edmonds, the superintendents, principals, and teachers in Michigan training program gained confidence and began to build expectations for success.

The results of the Michigan training demonstrate, as many researchers have maintained, that a change in attitudes and expectations does not necessitate a wholesale turnover in the staff of a school. Just as high expectations for students are a necessary precursor to change, so are high expectations for teachers. Lezotte maintains that the men and women who already work in schools are the best people to manage the process of change, and that they possess the capacity to do better in all of their professional activities. Turning around an ailing school requires staff members to "rethink what they are doing and the conditions under which they operate," Lezotte concludes.

Fear of cost. One potential roadblock to the spread of staff training programs is the cost. When budgets get tight, staff development can sometimes be perceived as a dispensable frill. Lezotte points out that the education community spends far less on training than private industry—an average of 2 percent of the total budget for education, compared with between 7 and 10 percent among industry.

The AASA survey revealed that, despite funding and attitude obstacles, innovative staff training is taking place from one end of the country to the other. In one Wisconsin community, a superintendent is using staff to solve professional problems and using community leaders to meet school building needs at low cost. A Long Island superintendent runs continuous training programs in new instructional methods for the entire district staff (and has also pulled the community together in a shared decision-making process). The result has been improved curriculum development. In Utah, one principal overcame what he characterized as a culture of "apathy to change" from teachers, staff, and community and started up a mastery learning program.

Mastery Learning and Expectations

Some teachers in buildings using an effective schools model found that even though they had high expectations and acted upon them, some students still were not learning. A recent body of literature has addressed this problem, recommending a range of promising techniques for assuring that all students achieve mastery. Most of these strategies require the entire school, and not just teachers, to embrace high expectations and develop specific strategies for students that are not learning as quickly as others. (See Chapter 5 for more on mastery learning.)

The concept of mastery learning is one such approach. According to Benjamin Bloom of the University of Chicago, mastery learning is based on the assumption that all children can learn the basic school curriculum, but it takes some longer than others. Bloom, a developer of mastery learning, maintains that most teachers begin a school year with the view that some students will learn well, some will learn only moderately well, and some will learn very poorly. By the end of the first month, says Bloom, teachers in most schools have mentally sorted their students and very effectively convey their opinions about student capabilities in subtle and not so subtle ways. Only rarely do teachers expect the majority of their students to learn well, Bloom adds; the unfortunate consequence is that most students come to accept the teacher's view of their own learning capabilities.

Most students come to accept the teacher's view of their own learning capabilities

When teachers use a mastery learning approach, whereby students begin with simple tasks and work up to more difficult "units' of information, both teacher and student attitudes improve, and learning increases, according to Bloom. Within four to six weeks under a mastery learning experiment, most teachers note improvements in achievement compared with conventional methods of instruction. At that point, Bloom observes, most participating teachers refuse to use a control group, on the grounds that it would be akin to denying a health-saving drug like penicillin to people in need.

The Historical Perspective

If the shift in attitudes called for by effective schools advocates occurs on a broad scale, it will be nothing short of a major change in the history of educational philosophy. Historian and educator Lawrence Cremin has examined the issue of expectations and brings an interesting historical perspective. "For most of human history," said Cremin, "men and women have believed that only an elite is worthy and capable of education and that the great mass of people should be trained as 'hewers' of wood and 'drawers' of water, if they are to be trained at all. It was only at the end of the 18th century and the beginning of the 19th that popular leaders began to dream of universal school systems that would give everyone a chance to partake of the arts and sciences.

"Not surprisingly, they had their most immediate successes with the children who were easiest to teach—those who, through early nurture in the family and other institutions had been prepared for whatever it was that the school had to offer.

"Now in the 20th century, we have turned to the more difficult task, the education of those at the margins—those who have physical, mental, or emotional handicaps, those who have been held at a distance by political or social means, and those who, for a variety of reasons, are less ready for what the schools have to offer and hence are more difficult to teach."

Teachers' Expectations for Themselves

Lezotte also makes an important point about expectations: student success, he says, must be "'launched' from a platform of teachers having high expectations for self." In addition, he notes, the school must assure that teachers have access to tools that will enable them to help all students learn successfully.

SOURCES

Averich, Harvey A. and others. "How Effective is Schooling? A Critical Review and Synthesis of Research Findings." Santa Monica, Calif.: Prepared for The President's Commission on School Finance. Rand Corporation, 1972.

Barnett, Homer G. *Innovation: The Basis of Cultural Change.* New York, N.Y.: McGraw Hill, 1953.

Becker, Marc S.; and Barry, Janet N. "School Effectiveness at the Secondary Level; The Glendale Union Model." *In Case Studies in Effective Schools Research*, pp.74-86. Edited by Barbara O.Taylor, National Center for Effective Schools Research and Development, University of Wisconsin., June 1990.

Block, J.H. "Mastery Learning: The Current State of the Craft," *Educational Leadership* 37, 2 (1979): pp 114-117.

Block, J.H. *Schools, Society and Mastery Learning.* New York: Holt, Rinehart & Winston, 1974.

Bloom, Benjamin S. *All Our Children Learning.* New York: McGraw Hill, 1981, (marks and grades, pp.6,18-19, 36, 99, 139, 212, 243) (earned through mastery learning, pp. 135, 165,170) (mastery learning, 126-128,153-174).

Brophy, Jere.E., Good, Thomas L. *Teacher-Student Relationships: Causes and Consequences.* New York: Holt, Rinehart & Winston, 1974.

Cremin, Lawrence A. *Public Education.* New York: Basic Books, 1984, pp. 85-86.

Edmonds, Ronald. *School Effects, Teacher Effects.* New York: Social Policy, 1984.

Katznelson, Ira; and Weir, Margaret. *Schooling for All: Class, Race, and the Decline of the Democratic Ideal.* New York: Basic Books, 1985, pp. 28-57, 83, 85-120.

Lezotte, Lawrence W. *Correlates of Effective Schools: The First and Second Generations*, 1989, pp. 3-4.

National Center for Effective Schools Research & Development. "A Conversation Between James Comer & Ronald Edmonds, Fundamentals of Effective School Improvement." Dubuque, Iowa: Kendall/Hunt Publishing Co. 1989, pp. 5, 6, 7, 8, 63.

National Governors' Association. "Strategies For Achieving The National Education Goals." Washington, D.C.: Task Force on Education, June 1990, p. 25.

Robinson, Glen R. *Learning Expectancy: A Force Changing Education.* Arlington, Virginia.: Educational Research Service, 1986.

Steller, Arthur W. *Effective Schools Research: Practice and Promise.* Bloomington, Indiana: Phi Delta Kappa Educational Foundation, 1988, p. 27.

CHAPTER 5: A FOCUS ON INSTRUCTION

"The acquisition of essential skills takes precedence over all other school activities."

— Mission statement of the Norfolk, Virginia, Public Schools

One Focus, Many Methods

It sounds like common sense: if the purpose of schools is teaching and learning, then instruction should be the hub around which all activities of the school revolve. Yet, when the effective schools pioneers posited this seemingly self-evident truth some two decades ago, they were motivated not by a desire to restate the obvious, but by research evidence and their own observations that in too many schools, the goal of instruction had become crowded out by a multitude of internal distractions and external demands. Extracurricular activities, personnel issues, community requests for social services—these and other activities can eat away at the time and energy available for teaching essential skills. Recognizing this problem, the effective schools advocates responded with a clear message: an effective school is one that has an unwavering focus on instruction, understood and accepted by everyone in the building.

As the administrators who responded to the AASA survey revealed, there are many reasons why instructional focus can become diffused, among them "teacher apathy" and "weakness in administrative leadership at the school building levels." At the same time, the survey revealed that administrators recognized the problem and were trying to do something about it. One upstate New York superintendent has mounted a "huge staff development program"; however, this administrator cautioned, "It takes years to get a program to the point where it makes a difference." A local superintendent in Kansas criticized the prevalence of lecturing in his district's classrooms and the absence of such instructional approaches as the Socratic method, even when teachers have been trained in its use.

Some Approaches for Improving Instructional Focus

Effective schools researchers generally steer clear of dictating particular instructional methods or strategies. Rather, they say, the methods should be determined by the school, and may vary according to participants, subject matter, and classroom objectives. A teacher's approach in the first period may well be put aside in the second period as students and needs change.

The National Governors' Association Task Force on Education agrees, to a point. "All students need a rigorous and challenging curriculum that teaches thinking, problem-solving, and the application of knowledge," the Task Force said. "However, decisions about how, where, and when teaching and learning best take place should be made largely at the local school level. To some extent, state assessment policies will shape school curriculum," said the task force.

Within this framework of local flexibility, effective schools research has highlighted some approaches that seem to yield success in improving student achievement and that complement the effective schools process. A common theme among these approaches is a strong caution about lecturing as the only instructional method and a strong encouragement of methods that more actively engage students in the educational process.

The Socratic Method

The direct questioning, or Socratic method, has garnered support among some effective schools practitioners. Under this approach, the teacher moves about the classroom and uses questions to help students reason out answers. It is especially effective in a seminar setting, in which students can engage in discussion, kept on course by the teacher or leader. Standing still in front of the room does not work well with this technique.

Coaching

Coaching is based on the notion that skills are acquired by habit formation. As John E. Roueche and George A. Baker of the University of Texas at Austin point out, "Good habits, which skills are, result from repeated acts under the guidance of a seasoned performer who is a coach." Teachers who "coach" build skills by supervising repeated student performances. In a more developed form of coaching, students who have grasped the skills in question can be encouraged by the teacher to coach their peers.

Madeline Hunter Model

Although it is part of the literature on teacher effectiveness and not on effective schools per se, the popular Instructional Skills program, developed by UCLA Professor Madeline Hunter at the same time the effective schools model was taking root, has been used with success in many effective schools. The Hunter approach requires teachers to check for student understanding before going ahead with instruction. If a student does not understand the instruction, then the teacher restructures the failed task and provides different examples and experiences to build the required background knowledge.

"It is important for teachers to check often for student understanding," said Jane Stallings of the Peabody Center for Effective Teaching at Vanderbilt University. "In group problem-solving tasks, those students who received an explanation after making an error solved the problem correctly. The explanation did not need to be directed toward a particular student but could have been directed toward any student within the same group. Those who did not receive explanations after an error were not able to solve the problem on a second effort." Stallings reported improvements in student attentiveness and achievement using the Hunter model. But, she also noted, student comprehension and understanding have not been tested, and research on the theory of understanding and the need for linkage is meager even though classroom results appear strong.

Mastery Learning

As noted earlier, mastery learning is another approach being widely used in effective schools. Under this approach, students learn highly detailed units of material by starting with easy tasks and moving up sequentially in difficulty. There are two principal formats for presenting the material. Teachers may present a unit to the whole class or students may work independently through the unit at their own pace. At the end of each unit, all students are tested. Those who do not achieve an 80 to 90 percent correct rate receive more instruction until they receive a mastery grade.

According to Benjamin Bloom, it is *time*, not native ability or entering achievement, that explains why some children in the early grades are not high achievers. Some students come to a new study unit with low motivation from previous failure and inadequate background information; these students fall progressively behind in achievement, and their attitudes become more negative. Bloom says the answer to the problem is to provide prerequisite skills and the time needed for all students to master the lesson—assumptions that dovetail with the basic ideas of the effective schools process. According to Bloom, once students in the mastery programs gain the prerequisite knowledge, they become increasingly faster in absorbing their tasks than non-mastery students.

Other researchers have identified some problems with mastery learning. Critics argue that using mastery learning for whole class instruction can impede faster learners. On the other hand, say some, allowing students to work at their own pace decreases the time for teacher instruction for each student.

Bloom counters that school districts involved in mastery learning continue to use the program and produce improved student test scores.

Cooperative Learning

The rationale behind the Cooperative Learning method is that to be successful in the family, workplace, and community, a person needs to know how to cooperate with others as well as compete. According to Johns Hopkins University researcher Robert Slavin, many classroom environments encourage competition rather than cooperation. Outside of sports, music and drama, few opportunities exist for students to develop their cooperative skills. Cooperative learning programs, developed in the 1980s, are intended to fill that gap.

Cooperative learning models vary. In some models, children work on learning as a group, using peer tutoring and other mutually supportive techniques. In other programs, the task is divided up and members of the group work independently, joining for help as needed.

Cooperative learning has its own rewards that are different from the individual, grade-oriented reward system prevalent in most classroom arrangements. In a cooperative program, the grade might depend on a product cooperatively produced by the group or the average of the student members' performance. Cooperative learning advocates believe that students can learn from each other, which benefits both high and low-ability children. The group reward structure is also intended to increase the motivation of low-ability students and teach all children respect for academic achievement.

Empirical evidence. Slavin conducted the most comprehensive study of cooperative education, which found that in a group of 53 third-graders, the cooperative learning students scored higher on a vocabulary and analogies test than students not in the cooperative program. In another Slavin study of 456 fourth- and fifth-graders, cooperative learning students scored higher than the noncooperative learning group on the mathematics computation section of the Comprehensive Test of Basic Skills (although not on mathematics concepts and applications section). Slavin also found positive effects on standardized achievement tests in four of seven other comparisons. Slavin and Nancy Karweit, a colleague at Johns Hopkins Center for Research on Elementary and Middle Schools, also found "positive effects" in measures of race relations, student perceptions of peer support, and mutual concern.

Cooperative learning sometimes aims at improving racial and cross-cultural relations in schools. By working together, advocates assume, children from different ethnic groups learn to appreciate each other's strengths and develop interracial friendships.

> Children from different ethnic groups learn to appreciate each other's strengths and develop international friendships

Service Learning

The National Center on Effective Secondary Schools at the University of Wisconsin, Madison, has been a leader in the concept of service, through the promotion of two models: academic service learning, which involves students from the upper elementary grades on, and community service learning, which is limited to high school students.

Academic service learning. In the academic service-learning approach, students who are experiencing academic difficulties are assigned to teach a group of students in a lower grade level. Anne Lockwood of the National Center for Effective Schools tells the story of Kate McPherson, a former classroom teacher in New York who is currently helping school districts in Washington State incorporate service learning into their curricula.

McPherson wrote that she "was struggling with an eighth-grade boy who could not read above the second-grade level and who was most comfortable when he failed because it was familiar to him.

"I was adjusting the reading level down as far as I could for the materials I had," McPherson explained, "but every time he was in a classroom there was a sense of failure. I tried every traditional instructional technique, but it wasn't really going anywhere. At that point my vice principal suggested that I have him tutor second-graders.

"I must confess, I was a little skeptical, but I have never seen a faster switch in my life. To those second-graders he was Mr. Jones, the teacher. It wasn't a technique of trying to make him feel valued; it was a genuine admiration that was coming from these little second-graders' eyes, that let him know he was needed for the first time. He'd always been needy, and a teacher had been helpful, but there were few opportunities for him in the classroom to be helpful. For many kids, it has so much powerful impact for them to be needed.

"For some kids," McPherson continued, "service learning provides a new context for learning that engages them so that they want to learn. The skills will follow, because of their engagement. In

Schools Team Up

Nichols Middle School and Dewey Elementary School in Evanston, Illinois, are among the many schools in the country that have tried cooperative learning with positive outcomes. According to the principals, Carmen Marcy of Nichols and Michael Martin of Dewey (Nichols' feeder school), the staffs at both schools "are fully committed." The proof, said Martin, "is reflected in the fact that 51 people attended the training sessions, which took five and one-half hours per week for six weeks—after a full day of teaching."

The program has reaped some visible benefits among students, too. According to Marcy, "Students share their talents and skills in a way that benefits everyone. In addition, they learn to like each other across potential barriers of class, race, ethnicity or handicaps."

Principals Marcy and Martin recommend several techniques for getting students started with cooperative learning, including these:

Continued

- **Reading groups.** Students read materials together and answer the questions. One person is the reader, another the recorder, and a third the checker, who makes sure everyone understands and agrees with the answers. The groups must come up with three possible answers to each question and circle their favorite one. When finished, the students sign the paper to certify that they all understand and agree on the answers.
- **Jigsaw.** Each student reads and studies part of a selection and teaches what he or she has learned to the other members of the group. Each then quizzes the others until satisfied that everyone knows all the parts thoroughly.
- **Homework checkers.** Students compare homework answers, discuss any questions or problems they have not answered similarly, then correct their papers and add the reason they changed an answer. They make certain everyone's answers agree, then staple the papers together. The teacher grades just one paper, and all group members receive that grade.

According to Martin, the program has enhanced partnerships among faculty, administrators, and the community, as well as students. "What's been most remarkable about the Dewey/Nichols program is the emphasis on 'partnership' at all levels," said Martin. "Cooperative partnerships solidified between and among Dewey and Nichols teachers and parents, vital community-school links, and the school-district-state network. All provide numerous benefits for the other key partners—our students."

terms of retention, kids tend to remember those sorts of applications longer. For a teacher it's enlivening. There's passion in the process, not just this sterile routine. And then I, the teacher, also learn."

Community service learning. Each day in communities across the country, a small portion of high school students—about 8 percent—are leaving school, not to drop out, but to clean up neighborhoods, visit with nursing home residents, educate young children about drugs, serve in soup kitchens, register voters, and serve their communities in many other ways.

Fred M. Newsman, director of the National Center on Effective Secondary Schools, reports that they do this not only with school approval, but with encouragement. About 27 percent of U.S. high schools support some type of service learning. Of these, about half offer it only as a voluntary club activity, 27 percent as an elective course for credit, and 15 percent as a graduation requirement. The mean number of hours per week students work in service is four, although in some programs students work more than 10.

Some programs, says Newman, try to integrate service opportunities into regular academic course work, but most function independently of the main curriculum. Experts in the field of service learning stress the need for involving students in responsible, challenging activities that have important consequences for the common good—and not as spectators, or visitors who do only routine, tedious tasks.

Mutually beneficial. Newman says that "impressive evidence from many schools and corroborating evidence from empirical studies show that service learning can contribute to the personal, intellectual, and social development of students from a wide variety of backgrounds."

Given these accomplishments, Newman wonders why so few schools have embraced the concept. The reason, he speculates, is not so much scheduling and logistical problems, but that service learning is mistakenly viewed as being irrelevant to the academic goals of high school.

"Most educators," he says, "have yet to be convinced that service learning can improve the teaching of English, social studies, math and science sufficiently to deserve the time and energy that such programs require . . . Major expansion of this movement will require service learning advocates to develop programs targeted more clearly on academic goals, and more flexibility from teachers in conceptualizing their course content. Neither of these will be easy to accomplish."

Nevertheless, Newman concluded, "Limited prospects for expansion should not be allowed to deflate the value of these programs. Even with a minority of schools and students involved, service learning can make a contribution to the lives of students and to the common good."

> Service learning can contribute to the personal, intellectual, and social development of students from a wide variety of backgrounds

Time on Task

In the AASA survey, principals and superintendents also talked of the need for more time—for instruction, for getting tasks done, for retraining teachers and administrators. As R.J. Matthews, principal of Luling Elementary School in Louisiana, wrote, "limited time blocks" for teaching was a major obstacle to effective instruction.

How teachers and principals use their time in the school building and the classrooms has been the subject of a great deal of research during past decades, and is the subject of an AASA publication, entitled *Time on Task*. The publication cites the research findings and the traps that teachers and administrators can fall into as they examine this complex issue and also publicizes some ideas for more meaningful use of time. For example, teachers can maximize instructional time if they come to class prepared with clear objectives for each day's lesson, develop a clearly understood classroom routine, and assign tasks that are appropriate to the time available. Principals, for instance, can do their part by minimizing outside distractions, such as bells and visitors, discussing problems with the staff, and keeping abreast of what is going on in the classrooms.

Basic vs. Higher Order Skills

Experts disagree about whether the effective schools movement, in its call for instructional focus, has placed too much emphasis on basic skills and not enough on such higher order skills as reasoning and analysis. For example, Lawrence C. Stedman, of the State University of New York at Binghamton, argues that too much drill and practice occurs in effective schools. Stedman based his point in part on a Massachusetts study, which "found that a majority of effective schools . . . had a very strong orientation to drill and practice" as a means of helping students master basic skills. Class time was often spent "having the entire group go over worksheets, or generally drilling students on basic skills," said Stedman, and little attention was paid to "how reading skills are used either to obtain and process information or to gain pleasure."

Does One Hurt the Other?

Nancy Borkow, a researcher with the U.S. Department of Education, found that emphasis on the basics has hurt higher order skills and brought down the test scores of higher achieving students. The National Assessment for Educational Progress attributed the decline in mathematics problem-solving skills that occurred during the 1970s in part to the back-to-basics movement. Stedman concurred: "Schools had spent so much time on computational skills that they had neglected analytical ones."

Stan Pogrow, professor of education at the University of Arizona, has examined the acquisition of higher order skills among at-risk children. He concludes: "The fundamental learning problem faced by at-risk children in grades four and up is that they do not understand 'understanding.' This means that many students have no conception of fundamental thinking processes, such as understanding the difference between guessing and using a strategy, or how to link ideas, or how to work with two concepts at the same time.

"This deficit," he points out, "results from a lack of conversation with adults that emulates the process of making inferences." Pogrow noted that, "We all know that schools are filled with children who never had a parent ask them to make an inference, and then help them with the process."

Basic Skills Lay the Groundwork

Others argue that basic skills provide the foundation on which higher order skills can accrue. Jane Stallings of Vanderbilt maintains that memory skills are essential for early elementary students to succeed in basic reading, writing, and numerical skills. Stallings explains that "memorizing facts increases students' ability to easily retrieve information from long-term memory, and this allows more space in the mind for understanding and problem solving. For example, the more automatic a student's memory of the times tables, the more mental energy can be devoted to problem solving as in word problems."

Developing Both

Many experts have attempted to resolve the debate by advocating a healthy mix of both basic skills and problem-solving skills. "The basics clearly have their place," says Stedman, but only as part of a rich academic program that engages students and then challenges them intellectually."

Some administrators, like Stephen Daeschger, superintendent of the Cedar Rapids, Iowa, Public Schools, are putting this into practice. As a second wave of effective schools implementation, his district is now focusing on both basic and higher order skills. Consensus about these instructional goals is exceptionally high and present in the schools to "a considerable extent," Daeschger said.

Broadening the content to be mastered by students presents challenges, particularly if the amount of instructional time (i.e., the length of the school day and school year) remains fixed. As with many reforms of the past decade, schools are being asked to do more with the same resources. Ultimately, suggests Lezotte, requirements for compulsory schooling might have to be reexamined.

Common Threads

The teaching approaches described above share some important characteristics that are relevant to the effective schools process. They stress the need for clearly defined goals and objectives. They recognize that students learn at different paces and that success in one task often depends on success in preceding tasks.

But, as their advocates emphasize, if these new approaches are to produce the most effective results, schools will have to make some significant changes in the way they are organized.

In *A Place Called School*, author John Goodlad states that at all levels of schooling, "curricular sameness characterize[s] the topical organization, factual organization, textbook content, and the things tested. The emphasis is on recall, not problem solving or inquiry."

Worth the Work

Roueche and Baker suggest that the school day format needs to change to accommodate techniques such as coaching and the Socratic method. A school day of rigid time periods, during which a teacher meets 120 to 150 students, encourages lecturing to cover the required syllabus, they conclude. Coaching, for example, demands one-on-one work between teacher and student; similarly, Socratic teaching is not simply questioning but also supplying the background "links" for what needs to be absorbed. Lecturing is easy, say Roueche and Baker. "It is far less demanding for both students and teacher, requiring less intellectual and physical engagement than other methods."

Mortimer J. Adler, a philosopher and professor at the University of North Carolina at Chapel Hill, director of the Institute for Philosophical Research, and honorary trustee of the Aspen Institute for Humanistic Studies, says that the Socratic approach and peer coaching methods require lots of training and take a long time for teachers to get comfortable. But, say Roueche and Baker, "they are skills; they can be learned; they can be polished by practice. And yes, some teachers will be more skillful than others, just as some are better at lecturing than others."

SOURCES

Adler, Mortimer J. *Reforming Education.* Edited by Geraldine Van Doren. New York, London: Collier MacMillan, 1990, pp. 293-317.

American Association of School Administrators. *Time On Task: Using Instructional Time More Effectively.* Arlington, Virginia, 1982.

Anderson, R.C. "Becoming a Nation of Readers. The Report of the Commission on Reading." Urbana, Illinois: University of Illinois, Center for the Study of Reading, 1989.

Arlin, Marshall. "Time Variability in Mastery Learning." *American Education Research Journal 23,* (1984): pp. 103-120.

Block, James H.; Burns, R.B. *Mastery Learning. Review of Research in Education (4).* Edited by S. Schulman, Itasca IL; and F.E. Peacock, 1976.

Block, J. H.; Efthim, H.E.; and Burns, R.B. "How Well Does Mastery Learning Work." *In Building Effective Mastery Learning Schools.* New York: Longman, 1989.

Bloom, Benjamin S. *All Our Children Learning.* New York: McGraw Hill, 1981, pp. 141-142,148.

Honnett, E.P.; and Poulsen, S.J. *Principles of Good Practice for Combining Service and Learning.* Racine, Wisconsin: The Johnson Foundation 1989.

Hunter, Madeline. *Increasing Teacher Effectiveness Training Program.* Los Angeles: University of California.

Hunter, Madeline. *Knowing, Teaching and Supervising: Using What We Know About Teaching.* Edited by P.L. Hosford. Alexandria, Virginia: American Society for Curriculum Development, 1984.

Lezotte, Lawrence W. *Correlates of Effective Schools: The First and Second Generations,* 1989, pp. 3-4.

Lockwood, Anne T. "Kate McPherson: A New Context for Learning." Madison, Wisconsin: National Center on Effective Secondary Schools, School of Education, University of Wisconsin, Newsletter 7 (Spring 1990): p. 6.

Madison, Wisconsin: National Center on Effective Secondary Schools, School of Education, University of Wisconsin. Newsletter 7, p. 1.

National Governors' Association Task Force on Education. "Strategies for Achieving The National Education Goals." Washington, D.C., July 1990.

Newman, F.M. "Introductory Remarks, Service Learning and Community Service for High School Students." Edited by Anne T. Lockwood, Spring 1990.

Newman, F.M.; and Rutter, R.A. "A Profile of High School Community Service Programs." Educational Leadership 43, 4 (1985/1986): 64-71 .

Pogrow, Stanley. "Solving The $4 Billion Mistake: Converting At-Risk Students into Sophisticated Learners." A paper presented to the Education Writers Association annual meeting, Washington, D.C., April 7, 1989.

Roueche, John E.; and Baker, George A. III. *Profiling Excellence In America's Schools.* Arlington, Va: American Association of School Administrators, 1986/1989.

Slavin, R.E. "Cooperative Learning and Student Achievement." *Educational Leadership.* Baltimore, Maryland, 46 (1988): 31-33.

Slavin, R.E.; and Karweit, N. Mathematics Achievement Effects of Three Levels of Individualization: Whole Class, Ability Grouped, and Individualized Instruction. Baltimore, Maryland: Johns Hopkins University, Center for Social Organizations of Schools, 1984.

Slavin, R.E.; Leavy, M.; and Madden, N.A. "Combining Cooperative Learning and Individualized Instruction: Effects on Student Mathematics Achievement, Attitudes and Behaviors." Baltimore, Maryland: *Elementary School Journal* 84 (1982): 409-422

Slavin, R.E. "Cooperative Learning." Review of Educational Research. Baltimore, Maryland 50, 2 (1980): 315-342.

Stallings, J. An Evaluation of the Napa County Office of Education's Follow-Through Staff Development Effort To Increase Student Learning Time and Achievement. Washington, D.C.: National Institute of Education, 1984.

Stallings, Jane. *Follow-Through Classroom Observation Evaluation, 1972-73.* Menlo Park, California: SRI International, 1984.

Stallings, Jane. "Madeline Hunter's Model. A Study of Implementation and Student Effects." Paper presented at the annual American Educational Research Association meeting, New Orleans, La., 1984.

Stallings, Jane. and Mohlman, G. "School Policy, Leadership Style, Teacher Change and Student Behavior in Eight Schools." Final report prepared for the National Institute of Education, Washington, D.C., 1981.

Stallings, Jane. "How To Change the Process of Teaching Basic Reading Skills in Secondary Schools." Final report to the National Institute of Education, Menlo Park, California: SRI International, 1979.

Stallings, Jane. A Study of Basic Reading Skills Taught in Secondary Schools. Menlo Park, California: SRI International, 1978.

Stallings, Jane. "Implementations and Child Effects of Teaching Practices in Follow-Through Classrooms." Washington, D.C.: Monographs of the Society for Research in Child Development 40 (1975): (7-8).

Stedman, Lawrence C. "The Effective Schools Formula Still Needs Changing. A Reply to Brookover." *Phi Delta Kappan* (February 1988): 439-442.

U.S. Department of Education, OERI. *What Works, Research About Teaching and Learning.* Washington, D.C., 1986., p. 7.

Webb, N. "A Process Outcome Analysis of Learning in Group and Individual Settings." *Journal of Educational Psychology* 15 (1980): 69-83.

CHAPTER 6: TESTING AND MONITORING PROGRESS

"What gets tested gets done."

— Ronald Edmonds

Appropriate and Inappropriate Use of Tests

The Debate on Standardized Assessment in Effective Schools

The role of assessment in effective schools has been frequently debated. Some researchers have criticized the effective schools movement for using paper-and-pencil tests as the key measure of school effectiveness. According to Thomas Good, for example, the reliance on standardized tests has helped to establish "a narrow definition of school effectiveness . . . There is no evidence that schools that teach the basic skills relatively well can also teach computer skills, science, and writing relatively well." Similarly, Lawrence Stedman made the point that tests that measure lower-order skills result in schools that are "narrowly structured to impart such skills."

The End Justifies the Means?

Effective schools researchers argue that while standardized tests are the instruments most commonly used by effective schools to measure student progress (just as they are in other schools), it is the use to which the test results are put that is important, not the test scores themselves. Ideally, testing is important to the effective schools process because it provides an indicator of whether mastery has occurred and a basis for modifying instruction if it has not. Unless schools use the results of tests and other types of assessment to inform decisions about instructional practices, the assessment becomes a routine exercise, an end in itself, and scores are not likely to change.

Against Sorting and Selecting

This view of assessment differs from the way testing is handled in some schools. Schools test students for a variety of reasons—to satisfy public demands for accountability, meet federal and state requirements, and sort and select students prior to the delivery of instruction. This latter reason is of particular concern to effective schools researchers, who advise against the use of tests to label students, choosing some for advancement while shunting the others aside. As Robert Lynn Canady of the University of Virginia and Phyllis Hotchkiss of Midwestern State University in Wichita Falls,

---

Counterproductive Testing and Grading Practices

To help teachers and administrators adopt fair assessment policies, Canady and Hotchkiss have developed a list of 12 all too common practices "that might be counterproductive for students at all ability levels":

1. Varying grade scales.
2. Worshipping averages.
3. "Zeroing" indiscriminately (i.e., giving students zero grades for such activities as not completing home work or or non-academic items like behavior).
4. Testing first, teaching later.
5. Failing to align testing to the curriculum.
6. Ambushing students with a "pop quiz," or "getting even."
7. Suggesting to a student that success is unlikely.
8. "Gotcha" teaching," or "read my pauses."
9. Grading first efforts, such as homework, when the child s initially learning.
10. Penalizing students for taking risks.
11. Failing to recognize measurement error.
12. Establishing inconsistent criteria for grading.

Texas, have noted, "One reason why schools have not been able to succeed . . . is that schools have been reluctant to give up their traditional roles of sorting and selecting." Add the researchers: "When 15 million children are at risk of academic failure and joining the ranks of the chronically unemployed, that time has clearly passed." Canady and Hotchkiss urge teachers and administrators to "shift focus from sorting and selecting to teaching and learning," so that all students can get a fair chance to be successful.

Good Intentions

To many civil rights proponents, standardized tests were originally seen as an impartial way to judge students. In Ronald Edmonds' original vision of assessment in effective schools, standardized tests had a clear place. Edmonds saw standardized tests as a way of bringing objectivity to the assessment process and had serious concerns about schools eliminating standardized tests in favor of measures that were too subjective. He was particularly concerned about ensuring fair assessment for disadvantaged children. "In the absence of standardized measures of pupil performance," said Edmonds, "school personnel are free to subjectively interpret pupil progress, and that interpretation is often misleading when low income children are the object of discussion."

Edmonds called the standardized achievement tests presently in common use, "a distinct improvement over historically subjective measures of pupil progress like teacher judgment." He went on to state, however, that standardized tests can only be defended because "they are in temporary use while we make greater progress in the design of criterion measures."

The master plan. Edmonds' ultimate goal was to use "locally generated, nationally validated criterion referenced achievement measures" as an appropriate instrument in effective schools. He explained his recommendation as follows: "I want these tests locally generated so that they measure what is being taught. I want them nationally validated so that the description of mastery in any district is accepted in all districts. And I want these tests to be criterion so that we know for each student whether or not mastery has occurred."

Overtesting. Edmonds did feel, however, that too much testing was occurring in schools. Testing should be cut by 50 percent, he said, calling for abolition of IQ examinations on the grounds that "there are no circumstances that justify such testing in any public school that I know of in the United States."

Researchers Speak Out

Lawrence Lezotte, Joan Shoemaker, and other effective schools researchers have been generally less positive than Edmonds about the usefulness of present-day standardized tests.

Lezotte has decried the lack of progress in developing more appropriate assessment instruments as "ten years of spinning our wheels." Lezotte continued, "We asked for reform and got standardized tests."

As Shoemaker has noted, "The trouble with these standardized, multiple choice examinations is that they do not truly measure what is being taught or being learned in our schools. Remember, they are produced outside our schools by firms that, because of what they do, almost dictate what is going to be taught," said Shoemaker. "That," she added, "is improper."

Hostile gatekeepers. These concerns mirror some of the criticism of groups such as the National Commission on Testing and Public Policy, which calls multiple choice exams "hostile gatekeepers," imperfect measures that have unfairly misclassified and limited opportunities for women, minorities, and many others. Moreover, notes George F. Madaus, the commission's executive director as well as director of the Center for the Study of Testing, Evaluation, and Educational Policy at Boston College, tests can have undesirable effects on instruction. "[I]f the evaluation procedures are designed and administered by an agency external to the school, rather than by the teacher," said Madaus, "then the procedures furnish the teacher with models of what they are expected to teach and what their pupils are expected to learn. This power of the tradition of past exams . . . has apparently been overlooked in the present rush by state legislatures to mandate minimal competency testing for high school graduation."

Reflecting the concerns of Madaus and others, the commission has urged schools and businesses to shift toward the use of alternative forms of assessment and to consider a broader range of information, including test scores, to evaluate students and institutions. Madaus is also conducting a study to determine if the testing industry should be regulated.

> The trouble with these standardized, multiple choice examinations is that they do not truly measure what is being taught or being learned ...

Disaggregating Test Scores

An issue that often arises in connection with assessment in effective schools is the question of whether scores should be separated out, or disaggregated, by factors such as race and socioeconomic status. In general, effective schools advocates believe that disaggregation yields important information about the relative progress of different groups of students.

Class consciousness. Key effective schools spokespersons have considered disaggregation of "extreme importance" (in the words of Lezotte), because it permits schools and districts to specifically identify academic achievement gains made by low-income and minority children. Without disaggregating achievement data, said Lezotte, "a school district could incorrectly interpret districtwide achievement gains as improvement among all children, when in fact, those gains were made only by some children, such as those from higher-income families." Edmonds concurred that school effectiveness was most accurately measured when disaggregated by social class.

Lezotte also emphasized that disaggregating achievement scores could be useful in exploring other concerns. For example, if the staff is interested in knowing whether a particular student's mastery of essential skills is related to attendance, they may look at the final data according to attendance groups, he said.

Most districts do not disaggregate scores, according to a 1989 report by the U.S. General Accounting Office (GAO). GAO found that during school year 1987-88, only 12 percent of the nation's school districts with effective schools programs regularly disaggregated academic achievement data according to student socioeconomic status, and only 9 percent broke down results by ethnicity. The GAO report concluded that disaggregation could be an important tool for determining the effectiveness of instruction for poor and minority children.

Teaching to the Test

Given Edmonds' observation that "what gets tested gets taught," one might logically raise the issue of whether, in an effective schools process, teachers would be pressured to "teach to the test." Edmonds and other researchers have made distinctions between teaching to the test and aligning tests with what had been taught and what had been learned. Other experts have cautioned, however, that holding teachers accountable for standardized tests results could give test developers undue influence over the curriculum.

Madaus, for example, feels it is imperative for course objectives and evaluations to be coordinated, as called for in the effective schools process. "The key to validity and fairness of evaluations is the extent to which they reflect the objectives of instruction," said Madaus. He urged that instead of the multiple choice tests, "many skills and competencies are better judged by more direct techniques: having the students write an essay, observing the student's performance in the science lab, listening to the student's pronunciation of a French passage . . . . "

Alternative Assessment

Cognizant of criticisms about standardized multiple-choice testing, school administrators are moving toward alternative forms of assessment, including various criterion-referenced examinations, performance-based assessment, and portfolio assessments.

Portfolio assessment is a form of subject-mastery exhibition in which students keep samples of their work for grades. A student portfolio might include everything that the student does in a specific subject over a designated period of time: completed homework assignments, test papers, essays, and notes taken during class. It could include extra work at the student's option, such as artwork

A Top Priority

The National Governors' Association Task Force on Education, in its 1990 report, says that states should "make the development of new assessment tools a top priority. New forms of student assessment are needed, tools that require students to synthesize, integrate, and apply knowledge and data to complex problems. These should present tasks for which no one answer is right, but for which a range of solutions may be possible. States should rely more heavily on essays, open-ended problems, portfolios, or other demonstrations of competence and accomplishment. These forms of assessment encourage active teaching and learning so that time allocated to the 'test' is not time away from learning. The research and development required to move forward on new assessments will be costly but worth the investment. Collaboration with other states can help reduce each state's share of the costs."

and comments on books read outside class, or the work that students feel represents their best.

Vermont is using portfolio assessment statewide; New York, California, Arizona, and Connecticut, all of which have large numbers of effective schools in operation, are considering this type of assessment. The Pittsburgh Public Schools have implemented a portfolio program. The National Governors' Association Task Force on Education has also urged that portfolio testing be considered on a wider scale.

Joan Shoemaker, director of school improvement programs for Connecticut and a fellow with the National Center for Effective Schools Research, says that alternative assessment "would not replace standardized tests" in the core subjects of English, math, science, and social studies, but would be a supplement to find out what the student has really learned.

Other experts have focused on the potential of technology—such as computerized practice tests, immediate feedback on homework, and computerized help with solutions—to enable teachers to better monitor student progress.

> The key to validity and fairness of evaluations is the extent to which they reflect the objectives of instruction

AASA Survey on Assessment Practices

A survey conducted by AASA for this publication revealed that 95 percent of the respondents use standardized tests, but nearly all use a combination of other testing methods as well to evaluate students. Of 128 respondents, 44 percent use oral examinations; 84 percent use teacher-developed tests; 66 percent use classroom observation; and 30 percent use other forms of assessment, such as portfolios, and exhibitions, such as special projects and term papers.

However, in a survey conducted for the 1991 AASA Critical Issues Report, *The Changing Face of Testing and Assessment,* over half of the respondents (51 percent) said that over the next five years they planned to expand their assessments to include criterion-referenced measures and performance assessments.

Accountability Cannot Wait

Several researchers and practitioners have concluded that although new kinds of testing tools are clearly needed, it would be a mistake for schools to suspend testing until better instruments are developed. Diane Ravitch, Assistant U.S. Secretary of Education, says that standardized tests will "continue to be pervasive unless some more objective means is devised." Continued Ravitch, "For teachers it is useful to discern grade patterns and [learn] where teaching needs to be strengthened." Ravitch called these tests "good early warning systems" for students, teachers, and schools, but she also warned that, "they are not perfect."

Interim Options

Marc Becker, research director for the Glendale Union High School District, Arizona, suggests that any school district not able to afford a good testing program should be able to inexpensively tap into the sophisticated statewide assessment programs that exist in states like New York, California, Connecticut, or Arizona.

The governors' task force urges states to "develop interim strategies for school accountability" until better assessment instruments are developed. "Holding schools accountable for student outcomes cannot wait," the task force explained. It listed three "interim options:"

• Continuing to use the current state assessment program.
• Adopting the assessment used by the National Assessment of Educational Progress.
• Requiring schools to develop and report their own accountability systems using locally-determined, results-oriented measures.

Each of these options, acknowledged the Task Force, is "less than ideal. The first sends the wrong message about the kind of outcomes that are needed, the second requires a substantial investment for a temporary solution, and the third does not permit comparisons of schools across the state." The task force concluded, "States will have to weigh the pros and cons of different approaches."

In 1992, the National Council on Education Standards and Testing called for the establishment of a new group, the National Council on Standards and Assesment, to consist of equal numbers of public officials, educators, and the public. The NCSA role, as they envisioned it, would be to establish guidelines for standard-setting and assessment development, among other duties.

Consistent with effective schools practices, the group emphasized that clear public standards for students must precede testing. Echoing another basic tenet of effective schools in its draft report to Congress, the NCEST called for recommendations of standards that would "reflect high expectations."

Sources

American Association of School Administrators. *Testing: Where We Stand.* Arlington, Virginia, 1989.

Canady, Robert Lynn and Hotchkiss, Phyllis R. "It's a Good Score! Just a Bad Grade." *Phi Delta Kappan* (September 1989): pp. 68-71.

Edmonds, Ronald R. *Testing and Educational Equity: The Status Quo and Prospects for the Future.* Speech at the Educational Testing Service Invitational Conference, New York, October 1981.

Educational Testing Service. *ETS Policy Notes 1, 2.* Princeton, New Jersey, March 1989.

Good, Thomas L., Brophy, Jere E. Brophy. "School Effects." *In Handbook of Research on Teaching.* Edited by Merlin C. Wittcock. New York: Macmillan, p. 598.

Hodgkinson, Harold L. "The Changing Face of Tomorrow's Students." *Change* (May/June 1985): pp. 38-39.

Lezotte, Lawrence W. "Base School Improvement on What We Know About Effective Schools." *The American School Board Journal* (August 1989): pp. 18-20.

Madaus, George F. *Introduction to Evaluation. All Our Children Learning.* Benjamin S. Bloom. New York: McGraw Hill, 1981, pp. 203-221.

Madaus, George, et al. *School Effectiveness.* New York: McGraw Hill, 1980.

National Governors' Association, Task Force on Education, Washington, D.C., June 1990, pp. 26,28-30.

Ravitch, Diane. *The Schools We Deserve: Reflections on the Educational Crises of Our Time.* New York: Basic Books, 1985, pp. 106-111, 119, 172-181.

Rothman, Robert. "Ford Study Urges New Test System To 'Open the Gates of Opportunity.'" Washington: *Education Week* IX, 36 (May 30, 1990): pp. 1, 12.

Stedman, Lawrence C. "It's Time We Changed the Effective Schools Formula." *Phi Delta Kappan*, (November 1987): p. 222.

U.S. General Accounting Office. "Effective Schools Programs: Their Extent and Characteristics," Briefing Report presented to the Chairman, Committee on Education and Labor, House of Representatives, Washington, September 1989.

U.S. House of Representatives. "Elementary and Secondary Education Conference Report To Accompany H.R. 5" (Report 100-567). Washington: U.S. Government Printing Office, April 13, 1988, p.83.

CHAPTER 7: PARENT AND COMMUNITY INVOLVEMENT

"The family is critical to success in school."

— The U.S. Department of Education

Parents' Vital Role in Effective Schools

Although the developers of the effective schools movement stress that the quality of home environment is no excuse for relegating certain groups of students to an inferior education, this does not mean that they have ignored evidence demonstrating the enormous influence of parents on the education of their children. To the contrary, effective schools advocates see parents as critical partners in the school improvement process. In essence, what effective schools researchers and practitioners are saying is that while family background is no excuse for poor schools, parental support and involvement in their children's education can be a significant asset.

Involving Parents

To foster this involvement, the effective schools model gives parents a meaningful role in planning and making decisions for school reform, and encourages schools to take active steps to promote parental involvement to the degree possible. As Mary Bicouvaris, a former teacher for 25 years at Bethel High School in Hampton, Virginia, and 1989 National Teacher of the Year, summed it up, "I know that nothing changes until parents and students get involved. Parents can and must help their children learn. We cannot let parents off the hook just because they are poor, have to work or don't have transportation. Schools must help those parents with special needs." Bicouvaris recommends that schools make extra efforts to reach parents who traditionally have not been active in the educational process:

Parental Involvement Can Make a Difference

The Orangeburg Public Schools in South Carolina are an example of how active parent involvement efforts can yield positive results. Although most of the 6,500 students in this semi-rural area are descendants of slaves and still live in poverty, more than half of the graduates of Orangeburg-Wilkinson High School enter college. School personnel and parents attribute this accomplishment in large part to the support for education that exists among Orangeburg parents. "Kids need a push from their parents," said Mattie King, whose daughter attends Rivelon Elementary.

James Wilsford, former district superintendent and the 1989 National Superintendent of the Year, believes, "You shouldn't sell a child short because of the house he or she lives in. I don't believe in blaming failing performance on young people because they are black or poor or from single parents. If the superintendent and teachers feel that way, the students and their parents will also. We don't only focus only on 'A'or failing students. There's a lot to be said for a 'C' student who works hard. He's going to be a good worker or a good parent."

Wilsford continued: "Some think that poor people don't care about their children. But as an inner-city high school principal [before coming to Orangeburg], I learned that although parents may never initiate a phone call to say they're worried about their kids, they usually respond when we call them."

Orangeburg has responded to a perceived need for parent training by running an early childhood parenting program in all its elementary schools. "Our teachers and counselors try to keep in close contact with parents at the middle and high schools as well," said Wilsford. "The PTA has high turnouts."

At Nix Elementary in Orangeburg, retired principal Irene McCollom recalled that in her first year, when parents did not cooperate when a child was continually unruly, "I put the kids in my car and took them home. The first year, I took at least five kids to parents at their jobs," she said. "Most parents cooperated after that."

"On back-to-school nights and teacher-conference days, schools should send buses into neighborhoods to pick up parents and bring them to schools. Teachers should schedule meetings with parents to accommodate the schedules of those who work. We must do everything possible to encourage parents to come to school to receive their child's report card. We must encourage employers to release employees for a few hours so that they can visit their children's school regularly. We must hold PTA meetings in housing projects, churches and community halls. We must show children that we value their parents."

School Improvement Teams

A Team Model

James Comer and Ronald Edmonds have agreed that parents need to be brought into the act before a school can truly be called successful. "I would argue," said Comer, "that if you create a climate which enables people to relate to each other with respect, and support each other, then you can better manage the stresses that are normal in school systems . . . . You must deal with the stresses that interfere with people doing their job."

The effective schools model pioneered by Edmonds brought parents to the decision-making table by reserving a place for them on the "school improvement teams." As Edmonds noted, "all parties to the organization have to be represented or you don't have a chance of advancing the agenda."

School improvement teams are a vital part of the effective schools process. Both Comer and Edmonds have said that the most effective teams should be limited to nine members and should include the principal, teachers, parents, and sometimes community leaders. In the high schools, the team might also include a nonvoting student representative.

In the model envisioned by the founders of the effective schools movement, parents would be full team partners who, along with other members, would sign off on an annual plan and be held accountable for school progress. To ensure that team members were more than rubber stamps for the school administration, Comer and Edmonds opposed the practice of principals appointing school improvement team members. As their experience demonstrated, appointed groups "were having enormously greater difficulties than the others." In actual practice, many existing school teams include a mix of appointed members, usually educators, and elected members, most often parents.

As conceived by the guiding researchers, the teams would develop a one-year improvement plan, then proceed to implement the goals and objectives of the plan. In real-life situations, teams have varying degrees of decision-making authority over budget, curriculum, and personnel. Usually each team is allocated a specific amount of discretionary funds per student, and team members exercise discretion in the choice of education programs, distribution of teachers across school programs, and selection of instructional materials. With respect to curriculum, decision makers at the school site might develop a new curriculum or modify or supplement the existing curriculum, based on the perceived needs and priorities of the school. Decisions might include selecting textbooks, choosing learning activities and supplemental materials, and deciding on alternative programs to be offered at the school.

Each team is ultimately responsible to the superintendent and staff, which must approve the school improvement plan before it becomes operative. In all cases, superintendents have oversight authority and can remove a team "for just cause."

Teams at Work in Real Settings

Some districts have given parents a strong voice on the teams, as envisioned by the effective schools pioneers. In the Lafayette, Indiana, Public Schools, school improvement teams, headed by principals, have wide latitude to manage a school's instructional and personnel allotments and to fund their own school's overall improvement plan, within the total budget allotment established by the central office. Teams also have authority to change school curriculum, said assistant superintendent Edward Eiler. As with most school-based management approaches, the superintendent of the Lafayette schools has approval authority over the team-developed plan.

In other districts, parents have been given a more limited role. In some cases, parents serve only as advisors when it comes to such educational decisions as curriculum, textbook selection, and teaching approaches. In some cases the authority to hire school staff rests solely with the principal. In other cases, teachers and the improvement team make recommendations, or actually make decisions, about screening, interviewing, and selecting staff persons. Some parent team members also carry out needs assessments for a school and serve as liaisons to the PTA.

In some school districts, a school's budget is prepared by the central district office and given to a principal and team to administer. Some central offices also screen textbooks before a school team can make its choices.

School-Based Management

A number of districts with active effective schools programs are also experimenting with the school-based management governance model pioneered in such places as Dade County, Florida. In these situations, the effective schools improvement teams and the school-based management teams, including parents, have become virtually synonymous. Where this type of decentralization exists, it is typically part of a district-wide school-based management effort, with teams in every school in the district. In addition to Dade County, several other Florida districts—Edmonton, Alberta, Duval County, and Monroe County among them—have made strides with the school-based management concept. The oldest operating

One Team Model

Delores Hardison, principal of Griffin Elementary School in Broward County, Florida, works with a school committee to put together an annual budget. Hardison heads the committee, which consists of teachers, other professional staff (including the school's budget planner), and parents. The role of parents on budget matters is an advisory one; however, Hardison says, "We listen to the parents very carefully, include them in our discussions, and consider their advice in our decisions. In that way, we are aware of their concerns and they are aware of our decisions." As regards decisions about buying textbooks, deciding on curriculum needs, hiring staff, and determining teaching, Hardison feels these decisions are the job of professionals. "Otherwise, why did most of us take six to seven years training? And after all, we are the ones being held accountable."

Hardison likes the local control that goes along with the school-based management process. "As long as I stay within the county and accreditation agency guidelines, I can shift my curriculum emphasis in any direction I and my staff feel necessary," she said. "Remember, each school has its own needs that differ from those down the road."

school-based management plan has prevailed in the Chesterfield, Missouri school district for 34 years. Jefferson County, Colorado, has practiced decentralized management for about 18 years.

Chicago Public Schools

One closely-watched school-based management effort is the massive experiment in governance being undertaken in the Chicago public schools. In an effort to revitalize an ailing system, Chicago established 11-member management teams—consisting of six parents, the principal, two teachers and two additional community members—at each school. The logistics of putting together teams in this district of almost 400,000 students are daunting—to fill the parent seats, the city held 542 local elections—and the transition to this new organizational mode has meant some disruption and confusion.

Chicago's school councils are responsible for a range of key decisions, including textbook selection, school improvement plans, discretionary spending, and hiring and firing of staff—including principals. State and central district office guidelines govern the operation of councils, which are under the supervision of the school superintendent. If a council fails to execute its duties, the central school board has the power to close a school.

Even though the controversial process has encountered some rocky patches, it has brought parents into the educational process to a degree never before seen in Chicago. One elementary principal of a school with a high percentage of children from families on public assistance said, "The election season has brought parents into the school who had never been in the building before and has invigorated students who felt that their parents did not consider school important."

> It just takes time for people to get used to each other and to work together. These are the first steps

The Need for Parent Training

Many parents, especially low-income parents, are not accustomed to interacting with the schools. Preparing parents to make the maximum contribution to the school improvement process may require additional support and training. Jeff Schiller, special assistant to the superintendent for Prince George's County, Maryland, Public Schools says, "it just takes time for people to get used to each other and work together. These are the first steps."

Instilling confidence. According to Patricia Dumont, principal of Riverside School in Lowell, Massachusetts, the Southeast Asian parents that comprise a high percentage of her community "shy away from leadership roles." To counter this problem, the school invited 10 parent representatives to work with administrators to plan for school improvement. Moreover, says Dumont, parents are members of the personnel selection teams. The upshot, Dumont says, is that at Riverside, parents are involved in the school "to a considerable extent."

A Feeling of Control

Prince George's County, Maryland, began a school-based management process with 20 schools the first year, and an additional 60 schools the second. The goal is to bring all schools into the process. Parent members of the teams must have children in the school they are representing; high school teams include student members. The purpose of the process is to provide schools with local spending control over their own effective school initiatives, said former superintendent, John Murphy.

To prepare team members to assume their roles as budget planners, the district requires each team to undergo a year of training. Training is continuous, as each new person joins a team.

"It is obvious that communities, specifically parents, become more involved in schools when they have some control over what goes on there," explained Professor Kent Peterson, director of the National Center for Effective Schools Research.

Obstacles to Parental Involvement

Challenges to School Systems

School improvement teams or school-based management teams have been a powerful force for giving parents a stronger voice in school affairs. Often, however, the parents who seek seats on school teams are those with records of active involvement in parent-teacher organizations or community affairs. The question remains as to how to get the majority of the parents of children in a school to work with teachers and other faculty to help their children improve academic achievement.

Schools with the best of intentions for involving parents often come up against several facts of contemporary life. Most of the parents have jobs, some even two jobs. Others lack transportation and child care for preschool siblings.

Involving minority parents sometimes means special challenges for school systems. James Comer observes that many minority parents are too embarrassed to come to school or take their child to a library because they are poorly dressed, do not speak mainstream English, or in some cases cannot read.

Deloris Hardison, a white principal in a largely black school, has developed ways of dealing with cross-ethnic challenges. "When I run into reluctance," she said, "I call a parent on the telephone until I contact them. I tell them I will come to them if it makes them more comfortable." Hardison said she also lets parents know from the beginning "that I am there to help them take care of their child, and I will do everything I can to help the child." Sometimes patience is required, Hardison said. "It takes a few years to gain the trust of the parents and the community. But it can be done."

> **I call a parent on the telephone until I contact them. I tell them I will come to them if it makes them more comfortable**

Parent and Teacher Perceptions

A study of eight urban elementary and middle schools, conducted by Joyce Epstein of Johns Hopkins University, found differences in perceptions among teachers and parents. Although almost all the teachers in the eight schools expressed strong, positive attitudes about the importance of parent involvement in general, many felt that if a parent was not involved with his or her child's school, it was because he or she did not want to become involved. Many parents in those same schools, however, reported that the school did not invite them to become involved. Epstein and her colleague Susan Dauber concluded that "parents are more involved at the school and at home if they perceive that the schools have strong programs that encourage parent involvement."

Differences in Attitude Among Teachers

Epstein and Dauber said that the way classrooms are organized influences school parent involvement practices. Teachers make more frequent and diverse contact with parents if they teach self-contained classes with limited numbers of students than if they are part of a teaching team or a departmentalized program in a middle or senior high school.

Teacher attitudes about parent involvement also varied according to subjects taught, said the researchers. Math teachers tended to be less willing than other teachers to attend evening activities; science teachers tended to be less active about informing parents of the skills required to pass their subject at each grade level; and social studies teachers tended to be less willing to participate in student-parent-teacher clubs and activities.

Parent Perceptions of Teachers

Parents give higher ratings to teachers who frequently try to involve them in their child's education, according to Epstein. Parents who are involved in their children's education at home or in school also say that when teachers work together with them, the school has a more positive climate.

Practical Ways To Involve Parents

Parents Working in Schools: The Comer Model

James Comer's approach uses parents as classroom assistants in their children's school. Under the Comer model, one parent in each elementary classroom works 10 hours a week at minimum wage. In addition, these parent assistants contribute many more hours in volunteer time. They help in social and academic areas, and they form the core of the larger parent group in the school. With the teachers and 20 or 30 other parents, they plan and implement a school social calendar based on the goals and objectives of the school management team.

Mutually Beneficial Learning

Parents in schools using the Comer model have developed workshops for themselves and other parents, usually led by building teachers and other staff members. These workshops are designed to help parents understand the academic and social programs of the school and learn how to help other children perform. "These activities were specifically designed to make the school a supportive place for staff members, parents and students," said

Parents' and Teachers' Perceptions of Several Steps That Would "Help A Lot" to Improve Education

Step	Parents	Teachers
	(Total) 2,011 %	(Total) 1,002 %
Having the school notify parents immediately about problems involving their children	88	77
Having parents limit television until all homework is finished	79	80
Having parents spend much more time with their children in support of school and teachers	70	84
Distributing a newsletter to parents about what's happening in school	68	51
Establishing a homework hotline students can call for homework advice	64	42
Having the school guide teachers more about how to involve parents better in the future	60	41
Getting teachers and parents to meet and talk about school policies	58	52

The Metropolitan Life Survey of the American Teacher 1987: "Strengthening Links Between Home and School."

Comer. "Activities include such things as a welcome back-to-school-dinner for orientation, the recruitment of new parents, and a graduation program to close out the school year with reflection and pride.

"Parents are also used in school for tutoring or in discussion groups where they can share their successes and their problems," said Comer. "Through these activities students can observe their parents—or people from the community who are very much like their parents—interacting in a cooperative way with teachers and other school staff members. Students often seek the approval, guidance and support of parent assistants in the building. And in a climate of good parent-teacher relationships, students are more responsive to the academic and behavioral expectations of the school staff."

Giving Parents Information

Parents in Joyce Epstein's study of eight urban schools said that they would become more involved if schools gave them specific information about their children's major academic subjects and about what their children are expected to learn each year. "They especially want clear information from the teachers at each grade level about how to help their children at home and how to monitor and assist with homework," she said.

Teachers in the Epstein study almost universally said that they expected all parents to fulfill specific responsibilities, such as teaching their children to behave, knowing what their children are expected to learn each year, and helping them with those skills. However, few teachers had practices in place to help the parents produce the desired behaviors at home, said Epstein. The study further showed that school programs and teacher activities to promote parental responsibilities varied widely among schools and between grades. Elementary school programs for parents, on the whole, were stronger, more positive, and more comprehensive than those in middle schools.

Epstein concluded, based on persuasive data, "that the school's practices to inform and involve parents are more important than parent education, family size, marital status, and even grade level in determining whether inner-city parents get involved in their children's education in elementary school and stay involved through middle school."

Fulfilling Basic Needs

Recent research has focused on developing practical approaches that parents can use, with or without a formal school parental involvement program, to help their children learn.

Professor Herbert Walberg of the University of Illinois suggests that parents:

- Provide books and a place to study.
- Observe routines for homework, meals, and bedtime.
- Limit the hours for after-school jobs.
- Discuss school events.
- Help students meet deadlines.

Questions for Parents To Ask Their Children's Teachers

Education researcher Kay McKinney of the U.S. Department of Education says that many parents feel uncomfortable meeting with teachers because they don't know what questions to ask. She offers some suggestions for parents who want to discuss curriculum, their children's progress, or things they can do at home to help. The questions were designed for parents of elementary school children, but many can be adapted for parents of middle and senior high students:

1. What are the teacher's academic goals for the year?

2. What will my child be learning in math or reading during the year? For example, in math will it be decimals, fractions, division, times tables?

3. Can I see samples of my child's work?

4. What must my child learn to be promoted to the next grade?

5. Are students placed in groups for reading or math? What group is my child in, and why? (Ask for specific reasons.) How often does the teacher reevaluate my child's placement in a group? If my child is in a low-level reading group and his skills improve, will he be promoted to a higher-level group?

6. What kind of tests does the teacher give to see if the students learned the material taught in class? How often are they given?

7. Are test results sent home or given to students?

8. What kinds of achievement tests will be given during the year? What is their purpose? How will the results be used?

9. How often is homework assigned? What role does the teacher expect me to play in homework?

10. How is my child's grade determined?

11. How often are report cards sent home?

McKinney has also developed a related set of questions parents can ask teachers to understand their children's progress:

1. Is he doing as well as he should be in school?

2. Is she performing at, above, or below grade level in her subjects?

3. S he completing homework assignments?

4. Does she need any special help in any subject? If so, where is the help available?

5. Does he get along with other children?

6. Does she show any behavior, such as squinting or being tired, that may signify a physical problem?

7. Does he participate in class?

8. How are her work habits and attitudes?

9. Can the teacher suggest ways I can help my child do better in school?

10. How does the teacher keep parents informed about children's progress or problems?

McKinney also suggests that this is a good time for parents to share information about their child. For example, have there been any recent problems in the home that may affect school performance? Parents can also take advantage of meetings with teachers to discuss any special talents, interests, or strengths their children show at home.

This is also a good time, McKinney says, to give the teachers a pat on the back. Frequently, the only time teachers hear from parents is when they have a complaint. Parents should make a point of complimenting the teacher when things are going well and of mentioning instances where the teacher has been especially helpful to the child.

Finally, McKinney has put together a checklist of questions for parents to ask themselves to assess how good a job they are doing supporting their children's education:

Questions for Parents To Ask Themselves

1. Do I attend parent-teacher organization meetings?
2. Do I read the notes and newsletters my child brings home from school?
3. Do I talk with my child's teachers regularly?
4. Do I keep up with his homework?
5. When my child brings home school work or regular homework, do I look at it and discuss it with her?
6. Do I read aloud to my child and encourage him to read?
7. Do I set high standards for my child, encourage her to do well, and praise her when she does?
8. Do I create a climate for learning in our home by setting aside quiet times for studying?

When both parents work, it is often difficult to find time for a school visit. Most teachers try to have at least one conference each year with parents of all their students, which usually lasts an hour or less. Recognizing this, McKinney suggests that working parents ask their employers to give them one hour off for a school conference. If that is impossible, the parent should arrange to talk with the teacher by telephone.

McKinney also recommends that parents who drive their child to school leave a few minutes early one day to allow time to stop in the school office, introduce themselves to the principal, and look around.

Parents who attend evening or weekend school functions, such as performances, plays, and sports events, call ahead and see if the teacher will agree to meet before or after the event. Some teachers may also be willing to come in early to meet before school. McKinney urges parents to remember that many teachers are also working parents who appreciate the scheduling problems involved. As McKinney says, if parents make the effort to meet with the teachers, most teachers will do likewise.

SOURCES

American Association of School Administrators. *Parenting Skills.* Arlington, Virginia, 1989.

American Association of School Administrators, National Association of Elementary School Principals, National Association of Secondary School Principals: *School-Based Management.* Arlington, Virginia, 1988.

American Association of School Administrators. *Building Public Confidence in Our Schools.* Arlington, Virginia, 1983.

Bicouvaris, Mary. "Education: Nothing Changes Unless the Parents Are Involved." *Virginian-Pilot,* Feb. 2, 1989.

Comer, James P. "Educating Poor Minority Children." *Scientific American.* 259, 5 (November 1988): 42-48.

Comer, James P. *Is 'Parenting' Essential to Good Teaching?* Washington: National Education Association, Families and Schools, 1988.

Comer, James P. *A Brief History and Summary of the School Development Program.* New Haven, Connecticut: Yale University, Yale Child Study Center, March 1988.

Comer, James P. "Parent Participation in the Schools." *Phi Delta Kappan.* (1986): 442-446.

Comer, James P.; and Haynes, Norris M. *Summary of a Plan To Expand Utilization of the School Development Program (Comer Process) Principles.* New Haven, Connecticut: Yale University, Yale Child Study Center (no date).

Dauber, Susan L.; and Epstein, Joyce L. "Parent Attitudes and Practices of Parent Involvement in Inner-City Elementary and Middle Schools." Baltimore, Maryland: The Johns Hopkins University, Report No. 33, March 1989.

Decker, Larry E; and Virginia A. *Home/School/Community Involvement.* Arlington, Virginia: American Association of School Administrators, 1988.

Epstein, Joyce L; and Dauber, Susan L. "Teacher Attitudes and Practices of Parent Involvement in Inner-City Elementary and Middle Schools." Baltimore, Maryland: Center for Research on Elementary and Middle Schools, The Johns Hopkins University, Report No. 32, March 1989.

Leslie, Connie. "Help for No-Hope Kids." *Newsweek* (October 2, 1989).

Lindelow, John; and Heynderickx, James. "School-Based Management." *School Leadership, Handbook for Excellence.* Edited by Stuart Smith and Philip K. Piele. Portland, Oregon: ERIC Clearinghouse on Educational Management, University of Oregon, 1989, pp. 109-134.

McKinney, Kay. *Parents: Here's How To Make School Visits Work.* Washington: U.S. Department of Education, Office of Educational Research and Improvement, 1985, pp. 4-7.

National Center for Effective Schools Research and Development. "A Conversation Between James Comer and Ronald Edmonds." In *Fundamentals of Effective School Improvement.* Dubuque, Iowa: Kendall/Hunt Publishing Co., 1989.

National Committee for Citizens in Education. *School-Based Improvement.* Columbia, Maryland, 1989.

National Committee for Citizens in Education. "Network: Parent Involvement in Middle Schools." Columbia, Maryland 15, 3 (Winter Holiday, 1989).

Powell, Douglas R. *Parent Education and Support Programs.* Purdue, Indiana: Young Children. Department of Child Development and Family Studies, Purdue University, March 1986, pp. 47-53.

Santoli, Al. "First Lesson: Believe in Yourself." *The Washington Post,* January 14, 1990.

CHAPTER 8:
MAKING IT HAPPEN

"If you are the local superintendent, you can make it happen. If you need to convince your school board it needs to be done, point to successes in other districts. In most communities, superintendents do not need convincing. Neither do most principals."

— Thomas Fitzgerald,
New York State Bureau of School Improvement

Defining the Mission

How can schools bring the effective schools process to fruition? The first step, according to those with effective schools experience, is for the school to define its mission, the primary purpose for its existence. This is best accomplished by bringing together people with a stake in the school and having them write a mission statement.

"It [the mission statement] is a good place to begin," said Gerald N. Tirozzi, Connecticut Commissioner of Education, "because the activity can be completed in a relatively short time, the activity requires the involvement of the total staff as well as parents and students, and the activity results in a tangible product that can be displayed in halls, classrooms and handbooks. Furthermore, this mission statement can serve as the driving force for instructional improvement."

Mission statements may differ widely among schools, districts, and states, although many reiterate some or all of the effective schools correlates. A mission statement can be as pithy as that of the East Detroit, Michigan, Public Schools: "All children can learn."

Or it can be as encompassing as that of the Norfolk, Virginia, Public Schools:

[The] focus [is] on teaching and learning and the belief that all children can learn; the principal is a strong administrative and instructional leader; the teachers hold high expectations for students in a caring, goal-oriented environment; the acquisition of essential skills takes precedence over all other school activities; frequent and thorough monitoring of pupil performance is required; community involvement is to be actively sought; and human, physical and fiscal resources are to be equitably distributed among the schools and tailored to students' needs.

> **A mission statement may change — perhaps should change — with time**

It can be framed in terms of expected outcomes, as the Alma, Michigan, school district did when it said that all students, regardless of family background, socioeconomic level, or gender, will achieve "mastery of the essential objectives in each subject area or course. Each student is encouraged to achieve to his/her highest potential."

Or it can be framed in terms of process, like New York State's mission: "To develop and support the leadership and local capacity necessary to assure high levels of achievement for all students of school age . . . ."

The evolution of a mission statement can extend over a period of years, as the input of new supporting players is sought. The Prince George's County, Maryland, statement evolved over three years, with participation of principals, teachers, parents, and community leaders. As this experience shows, a mission statement may change—perhaps should change—with time.

New York: A Case Study

New York State's Effective Schools Consortia Network helps districts and schools throughout the state develop "comprehensive school improvement plans," as the effective schools process is known in that state. The Network also serves as a clearinghouse for information on effective schools. (The consortium is an outgrowth of the effective schools efforts implemented in 1982-83 in Spencerport, New York.) Although the state does not mandate school improvement plans, a large number of districts and schools have developed them voluntarily, according to Deputy State

Commissioner Gerald L. Freeborne. Because of the state's involvement with effective schools and the work it has done to make the process understandable to local school districts, the New York State experience provides a useful frame of reference for the remainder of the chapter.

Establishing Goals and Standards

Once the mission is established, the school must define its goals—the results it expects to achieve for students and the school as a whole—and the quality and equity standards it will use to evaluate school improvement.

New York State set four very precise goals for its school improvement program:

1. Ninety-five percent or more of all students at each (grade) level demonstrate minimum academic mastery. Students who achieve minimum academic mastery have been prepared so that they will be predictably successful in the next grade in either their own school or in any other school building in the nation.

2. There shall be no significant difference in the proportion of youth demonstrating minimum academic mastery as a function of socioeconomic class.

3. The above two conditions shall be obtained for not less than three consecutive years.

4. Excellence will be represented by an increase in the number of students scoring in the upper three stanines on achievement tests. (In New York this also includes the number of students taking and passing state Regents' exams, which are criterion-referenced tests for individual subjects.)

Writing School Improvement Plans

Developing a plan to implement goals is an absolutely critical step, and one that entails more than inviting a group of people to sit down and draft a document. The guidance New York State provides its school districts describes the following stages of the process:
• Orienting school board members, administrators, teachers and teacher associations, parents and the community.
• Training key players in effective schools research.
• Engaging the district's commitment to the process by obtaining the approval of the superintendent and school board.

- Selecting school improvement teams.
- Assessing the school's needs by examining disaggregated student data, developing a comprehensive assessment report, and evaluating the effectiveness of the current instructional program. (Collecting baseline data from several sources can help a team better assess and define building level needs.)
- Developing the school improvement plan and seeking the review and endorsement of the faculty and superintendent.

Everyone who will be helping to put the school improvement plan into effect should be involved in creating the plan

Lawrence Lezotte says that everyone who will be helping to put the school improvement plan into effect should be involved in creating the plan. He emphasizes that the school board and superintendent should be involved and that ideally the superintendent would appoint a systemwide coordinating committee consisting of central office personnel, building-level administrators, teachers, and others.

Representation across the board. According to the New York State guidelines, team membership should be representative of staff, teachers, teacher associations, administrators (including the principal), and the community (including parents). Special education and compensatory education teachers should also be represented on teams. The aim should be to produce a three- to five-year plan that includes goals, measurable objectives, and activities that reflect faculty participation.

Even though components of a systemwide plan may vary, Lezotte says most take into account 11 features:

1. School system demographics.
2. Mission statement.
3. Communication within the system.
4. Communication within the community.
5. Curriculum.
6. Testing linked to the curriculum.
7. Timely availability of data to teachers.
8. A heavier investment in staff development.
9. Use of the school system plan to detail the rules under which individual schools must operate, including time cycles, needs assessment forms, and time available for staff planning.

10. A change of staff evaluation procedures to bring them in line with the reforms and make the transition from old to new procedures.

11. A decision on who will monitor the school system's progress (keeping in mind that those who wrote the plan may not be the most objective).

New York State has some additional tips to ensure that the planning process is representative and meaningful. The state guidelines suggests that the planning team:

- Collect pupil performance data and perceptions from the entire faculty and the community.
- Determine strengths, priorities, goals, and training activities for students, teachers, and staff.
- Identify timelines, responsibilities, and evaluation procedures.
- Prepare minutes of meetings or keep an "action record" and share the information with all school building personnel.
- Complete a written plan and share the draft with faculty and community.
- Document and evaluate each step in the process.
- Guide the implementation of the plan while revising it as needed based on faculty participation.
- Provide the superintendent and school building personnel with periodic reports on the implementation of the action plan in their building.

Implementing the Plan

It must be remembered that implementation takes time. As Gerald Tirozzi noted, "Increasing parent involvement, raising expectations, and providing increased opportunities to learn require longer periods of time and may involve staff development and other resources . . . . Action plans addressing improved achievement and instruction extend beyond one or two years and require the greatest concentration of time and resources."

East Detroit, for example, worked with the effective schools process for several years before "it brought focus and structure to the efforts of all in the district," said assistant superintendent, Emil Ciccoretti. But the results were worth the time and energy, he said. Genuine changes have occurred in the schools. "All children are offered a 'rich' curriculum, as opposed to reserving enrichment for a select few," Ciccoretti noted. "The former 'gifted' program has been restructured into an enrichment program available to all students through the regular classroom and through after-school opportunities."

Support and resources from the district, state, and other sources are essential to implementation, as is a timeline of activities to be completed within specified periods. Lezotte proposed that school boards find a place and time for the school teams to meet regularly, recognizing that time is "the code word for money—and money is something you never have enough of." He emphasized that board members should also learn the language of the effective schools process so that all will meet on common ground.

Evaluating Progress

As effective schools efforts expand, assessment of progress has taken on increasing importance. Typically student achievement data is the primary source for evaluating the success of a school. To judge the quality of the program, most schools look at total school performance on standardized tests. In New York, student test data are reviewed every three years, along with other trend data, including enrollment, attendance, dropout rates, racial and ethnic distribution of pupils, average class size, the ratio of students to support staff, student socioeconomic status, and pupil mobility.

To judge equity, many effective schools compare achievement scores and other measured results disaggregated by group.

The "Why" Behind the "What"

Some practitioners have expressed concern that test scores do not tell the whole story. As New York effective schools coordinator Thomas Fitzgerald has remarked, test data can tell a school what happened, but "it tells us nothing about why.

"Why, for example," said Fitzgerald, "are reading scores above average at one grade level and below at another? Why are math scores above average in one elementary building and below average in another?"

As a supplement to pupil test data, researchers and practitioners have produced other instruments to assess progress and trends in effective schools. One such instrument is New York's program assessment scale, which provides the teaching staff with a means to rate instructional programs using eight criteria:

1. Curriculum—sequence, definition, development, and alignment with the tests to be used.

2. Student placement.

3. Student monitoring.

4. Coordination and articulation between grades.

5. Coordination between school buildings.

6. Coordination of special education, other special services, and regular programs.

7. Evaluation.

8. Staff involvement.

Assessment Instruments

In addition, effective schools personnel have developed surveys to help assess the perceptions of teachers, other staff, parents, and students. The "Survey of Professional Staff Perceptions of School Program" developed by the New York State Education Department draws upon effective schools research and research about effective instructional practices. Comparable surveys have been developed to collect perception data from parents and students.

Among the test instruments used widely is the Connecticut School Effectiveness Questionnaire. This 73-item questionnaire was used by Edmonds and Lezotte to set up the Spencerport school profiles and the original New York State plan. In addition, 22 school districts in Michigan used it in 1983 to find out if the effective schools process correlates were in use and, if so, how widely, reported Lynne Benore, project coordinator for Michigan's Middle Cities Education Association. In 1986 the Michigan districts used the questionnaire again as a post-test to measure effectiveness.

Effective schools implementation is best viewed as a cyclical process, not a straight line

Revising the Plan

Effective schools advocates generally agree that an integral part of the process is making adjustments in the plan and timelines as needed. "The school improvement plan is just that—a plan," says Thomas Fitzgerald. "The school team should periodically review the plan and, if necessary, revise it to reflect the priority needs of the school."

New York recommends that teams go through the entire process every year. In all cases, the team should keep the superintendent and school building personnel informed of any revisions.

Thus, effective schools implementation is best viewed as a cyclical process, not a straight line. Making it happen—and continue to happen—requires constant vigilance, dedication, and recommitment to the process.

SOURCES

Bennis, Warren; and Nanus, Burt. *Leaders: The Strategies for Taking Charge.* New York: Harper & Row, 1985.

Benore, Lynne. "Middle Cities in Michigan. Twenty-Eight Urban Districts Across Michigan." *In Case Studies in Effective Schools Research.* Edited by Barbara O. Taylor. Madison, Wisconsin: National Center for Effective Schools, University of Wisconsin, 1990, pp.180-192.

Buffone, Joan; and Ciccoretti, Emil. "The Effective Schools Program in East Detroit Public Schools." *In Case Studies in Effective Schools Research.* Edited by Barbara O. Taylor. East Detroit, Michigan: National Center for Effective Schools, University of Wisconsin, Madison, 1990, pp.97-105.

Carter, Gene R.; Madison, Ann B. et al. "A Case for Equity and Quality: How One Team Is Making It Happen." *In Case Studies in Effective Schools Research.* Edited by Barbara O. Taylor. Norfolk, Virginia: National Center for Effective Schools, University of Wisconsin, Madison, 1990, pp.36-51.

Coleman, J.S.; Hoffer, T.; and Kilgore, S. *Public and Private High Schools: The Impact of Communities.* New York: Basic Books, 1987.

Coleman, James S.; Hoffer, Thomas; and Kilgore, Sally. *High School Achievement.* New York: Basic Books; 1982.

Corcoran, Thomas B. "Effective Secondary Schools." *In Reaching for Excellence: Effective Schools Sourcebook* (ED 257 837). Edited by Regina M.J. Kyle. Washington, D.C.: National Institute of Education, 1985.

Crowder, Bruce H.; and Fitzgerald, Thomas P. *New York State School Improvement Guidebook.* Albany, N.Y.: New York State Education Department, (no date).

Goodlad, John I. *A Place Called School: Prospects for the Future.* New York: McGraw Hill, (ED 236 137) 1984.

Lezotte, Lawrence W. "Base School Improvement on What We Know About Effective Schools." *The American School Board Journal* (August 1989).

McKinstry, William R.; and Gibbs, George R. "Alma Public Schools." Alma, Michigan: *In Case Studies in Effective Schools Research.*Edited by Barbara O. Taylor. Madison, Wisconsin: National Center for Effective Schools, University of Wisconsin, Madison, 1990, pp.49-51.

Murphy, John A. "Steps to Improvement in Prince George's County Public Schools"; "Part I, Effective Schools: A Total Commitment"; "Part II, Strengthening the School Improvement Process Through School-Based Management." Upper Marlboro, Maryland, July 1989.

Oakes, Jeannie. *Keeping Track: How High Schools Structure Inequality.* New Haven, Connecticut: Yale University Press, (ED 274 749) 1985.

Prince George's County Public Schools Division of Instruction. "Summary of Instructional Initiatives Designed To Ensure Successful Learning Experiences for Students in Prince George's County Public Schools." Upper Marlboro, Maryland, January 23, 1990.

Sudlow, Robert E. "Implementing Effective Schools Research in Spencerport, New York." *In Case Studies in Effective Schools Research.* Edited by Barbara O. Taylor, Madison, Wisconsin: National Center for Effective Schools Research, University of Wisconsin, 1990, pp.154-179.

Tirozzi, Gerald N. "The School Effectiveness Report: History, Current Status, Future Directions." Hartford, Connecticut: A report to the Connecticut State Board of Education, February 7, 1989.

Tomlinson, Tommy. M.; and Walber, Herbert J. *Academic Work and Educational Excellence: Raising Student Productivity.* Berkley, California: McCutchan, 1986.

Waynant, Louise F.; and Murphy, John A. "Reaching For Excellence and Equity In Prince George's County Public Schools," *In Case Studies in Effective Schools Research.* Edited by Barbara O. Taylor, Madison, Wisconsin: National Center for Effective Schools Research, University of Wisconsin, June 1989, pp. 12-35.

CHAPTER 9: EFFECTIVE SCHOOLS TODAY AND TOMORROW

"Make no mistake, research and knowledge of the best available practices do not give all the answers . . . . There remains much to be done, but it is true that research tells us that some things do tend to work better than others, and they represent a place to begin the improvement journey."

— Lawrence Lezotte

New Implementation Issues

The Impact of Broad School Reform Efforts

Much of the recent impetus for effective schools has come from broader school improvement initiatives undertaken by local school districts, state education agencies, governors, regional accrediting associations, and the federal government. The school reform movement of the 1980s and the newest proposals ensuing from the national education goals for the year 2000 embraced by the Governors and the White House have helped place the effective schools concept within a larger "legal, political, and organizational setting," according to Lawrence Lezotte, and has resulted in a "new, stronger formulation of the effective schools process."

Local Efforts

As described in previous chapters, some of the earliest school reform efforts incorporating effective schools correlates were undertaken by major urban school districts, such as Chicago,

Milwaukee, Minneapolis, New York, San Diego, St. Louis, and Washington, D.C. Often these districts were responding to local or internal demands for school improvement and found themselves grappling with difficult issues, such as developing a workable combination of central office support and school-site control. Many of these local programs are now well-accepted parts of overall district improvement efforts. According to Lawrence Stedman, local parent and community groups often assess school performance using effective schools checklists. There is also some evidence that these efforts have contributed to what the Council of Great City Schools calls "a clear trend of rising scores in large-city districts over the past five years."

Urban reform is just one component of a much broader movement; rural and suburban schools have also adopted improvement strategies based on effective schools research, and many can point to positive results.

State Programs

States have been major players in promoting effective schools research. Many state departments of education have created statewide effective schools programs or built effective schools concepts into ambitious reform packages focused on achieving the national education goals. The Connecticut Effectiveness Project, the first statewide attempt to systematically apply effective schools research, provides state-level technical assistance to help schools voluntarily implement school effectiveness characteristics. Mississippi's Education Reform Act, for example, includes a directive that all children "are expected to achieve mastery." Michigan requires school improvement plans, based on effective schools research, for every school, and also provides state incentives for effective schools. South Carolina, for example, requires each school to have a school improvement council, modeled after the councils recommended in much of the effective schools literature, to assess school needs and implement and monitor school improvement plans.

The current group of statewide programs share several characteristics. Most are voluntary and rely heavily on school-level initiatives and local planning. Many provide technical assistance, evaluate programs, analyze data, train staff, and disseminate information to help local districts through the process. North Carolina and West Virginia, for example, are among the states that support leadership academies to improve skills of school principals. Many states also reward schools that show progress toward effectiveness with monetary grants or waivers of state rules and regulations.

Using Effective Schools Research in Accreditation

Most recently, state and regional accrediting agencies have begun examining ways to encourage change by building effective schools correlates into their elementary and secondary school accreditation requirements. The Texas Education Agency, for example, has incorporated effective schools research into its statewide accreditation efforts and is continuing to explore ways to use effective schools correlates to guide on-site accreditation reviews. A number of other states—such as Michigan, North Carolina, South Carolina, Connecticut and Maryland—as well as regional accrediting associations, are implementing or considering programs linking accreditation with effective schools concepts. The thrust of these initiatives is to move the accreditation process away from examining only educational inputs, such as teacher-student ratios and number of credit hours—and toward a consideration of desirable outcomes, such as improved student performance.

Federal Support for Effective Schools

The 1988 Hawkins-Stafford Elementary and Secondary School Improvement Amendments, Public Law 100-297, gave a boost to the effective schools movement by reserving a percentage of funds for initiating and expanding effective schools programs under the Chapter 2 program. Chapter 2, which had provided relatively unrestricted block grant funding for states and local districts to use as they saw fit, was revised in the Hawkins-Stafford law to narrow its purposes and focus the money more clearly on school improvement. A set of key amendments, sponsored by Congressman Augustus F. Hawkins, former Chairman of the House Education and Labor Committee, required state departments of education to spend at least 20 percent of the state-administered portion of Chapter 2 funding for "effective schools programs"—defined in the Act in a way that embodied Edmonds' five correlates. These earmarked funds could be used by states to plan, implement, support, evaluate, revise, and strengthen effective schools programs, either through grants to local school districts or through statewide activities, such as technical assistance.

This amendment resulted in an infusion of several million dollars annually for effective schools. The state-administered portion of Chapter 2 amounts to about 20% of the total appropriation—

states must pass through at least 80 percent of their appropriations to local school districts—so the share for effective schools is 20 percent of 20 percent, or 4 percent of the total.

Emerging Challenges of School Reform

On one hand, the intertwining of effective schools research with broader school reform initiatives makes it more difficult to continue to view the effective schools process as an isolated concept. On the other hand, it suggests that effective schools research has gained wide acceptance and, in at least some places, has become institutionalized.

The vigorous activity in implementing effective schools processes at the local, state, and federal levels has raised new implementation challenges. In certain situations, local schools find themselves struggling to achieve their visions of schoolwide reform while remaining in compliance with federal and state mandates. Some researchers have also cautioned that the emphasis on test-based achievement results and the establishment of stricter state standards could have the effect of narrowing the definition of an effective school or of increasing the sorting and classification functions of schools. In addition, the identification of "ineffective" schools by states, using accreditation standards or other means, raises the issue of whether the schools identified will receive adequate resources and other support needed to improve.

> The identification of "ineffective" schools by states ... raises the issue of whether the schools identified will receive adequate resources and other support needed to improve

New Research Needs

A Vibrant Climate

These and other questions arising from the maturing of the effective schools movement suggest directions for new research, pilots, and models. Effective schools researchers are responding. In schools of education, education research laboratories, and elementary and secondary school buildings around the nation, contemporary researchers are investigating ways to expand or reshape the effective schools model to address fresh situations, such as how to improve suburban and rural schools and high schools. Some education professionals, such as Gordon Cawelti, the executive director of the Association for Supervision and Curriculum Development, are rethinking the basic correlates to eliminate what Cawelti terms "biases that have crept into the effective schools process."

How it fits. Several people are examining the relationship between the effective schools process and a growing body of related, independently-developed school reform approaches, such as time on task, active learning, other effective instructional practices, and school climate studies. One current focus is the relationship between the effective schools process and new efforts to promote teacher effectiveness, such as cooperative learning, higher teacher expectations, and mastery learning. According to Barbara Taylor, of the National Center for Effective Schools, "Effective schools and effective teaching are complementary literatures in the field, and they intersect at classroom management concepts."

> **The effective schools movement appears to have started a number of reform balls rolling**

At the same time, a number of research and demonstration efforts are underway which, although not extensions of effective schools research per se, owe a debt to the effective schools literature. By focusing attention on the need to thoroughly restructure individual schools, the effective schools movement appears to have started a number of reform balls rolling.

The result is a vibrant climate of activity and interaction among researchers and practitioners. Described below are a few of the more promising new areas of research that are extensions or offspring of effective schools literature, as well as some unresolved issues related to effective schools that invite further research and experimentation.

Effective High Schools

The Need for Reform

As noted in earlier chapters, the original focus of the effective schools movement was the elementary school; in the mid-1980s, the process was expanded to encompass middle schools. Although the process is currently being used by several hundred high schools, there have been few comprehensive studies to assess its effects at the high school level. Given the significant differences between high schools and primary schools—their larger size, their departmentalization by subject—it is not surprising that effective schools researchers and critics, including Edmonds, have warned that generalizations based on studies of elementary schools should be applied with caution in secondary schools.

This is not to say that high schools could not benefit from systematic reform. A host of education reform commissions, including several panels of business people concerned about the long-term effects of educational stagnation on American competitiveness, have underscored the need to improve American high schools. The National Governors' Association education task force has called for "radical changes" at the state level, acknowledging, however, that "state policies cannot mandate the necessary changes from the top. But fundamentally altering the policy environment in which all schools operate can provide the incentives and build the capacity for dramatic improvement at the bottom."

Much talk, little action. Many researchers agree. Fred Newman, director of the National Center on Effective Secondary School Research at the University of Wisconsin, Madison, noted that while "high schools are doing their job about as well as they've ever done with students who really want to succeed in school . . . [t]hey continue to fail the large proportion of students who don't buy into the standard school rituals." Newman added that with all the public pressure during the past decade to reform education, there would be more activity. "But," said Newman, "we don't notice major changes in the way schooling is conducted on the grand scale even after all the national huffing and puffing and report on report."

One possible reason for the lack of activity, said Newman, is the existence of organizational habits "that are very hard to break out of, like teachers accustomed to 125 kids a day and 5 classes a day, each 50 minutes in length and with a standard curriculum." According to Newman, "high schools have learned how to function rather well, not necessarily from the kids' point of view but in terms of making it through the day following traditional forms of curriculum, teaching and testing. There really haven't been many opportunities to see alternative models work."

Newman also pointed to the fact that, "Many people simply aren't convinced of the need to do things differently. After all, we are graduating kids from high school at high rates, kids are going onto college, the buses are running, and in most of the schools in the country you don't find any visible serious problems."

Overwhelming odds. The need for reform is particularly critical in inner city schools with large proportions of disadvantaged students. But as Albert Shanker, president of the American Federation of Teachers says, when you try to talk about change in the urban areas, the basic response is that things are so bad and the system is so complicated that it's hopeless to try to do anything.

Newman elaborated on this mindset: "In the most visibly troubled schools," he explained, "you have a sense of despair that prevents any new approaches to change. In the more affluent schools, people don't perceive the need for significant changes."

> In the most visibly troubled schools, you have a sense of despair that prevents any new approaches to change

Types of Reform Needed

The biggest problem with American high schools, according to Theodore R. Sizer, professor of education at Brown University and chairman of the university's Coalition of Essential Schools, is that they try to teach too much. Sizer is one of the leading researchers attempting to adapt some of the effective schools concepts to senior high schools.

"American high schools [are] similar to shopping malls offering a confusing array of fact boutiques of varying quality," said Sizer. "One store (or class) sells historical dates, personalities and incidents; the other, chemical tables; the other, fictional characters, authors and literary forms. The rich contextual framework needed to knit together these isolated pieces of information cannot be supplied in such a setting.

"There is little opportunity for synthesis in such disjointed presentation," Sizer maintained. "Of course, as in the shopping mall, the student chooses whether to buy. While that may happen in the traditional classroom, it's far less likely to happen where the focus is on the student as worker."

Shouldering a heavy load. Another problem highlighted by Sizer is the heavy teaching loads most high school teachers must contend with. "When I walk into a school and am told the great things they are doing, the first thing I ask is: 'What is your teacher load?' With 130 kids a day, no change will take place. With 120 to 175, that's too many kids. If you agree with me that no two kids are alike and each learns differently, I ask: 'How many can you teach at once?'"

Read between the lines. Fred Newman agrees with many of Sizer's points and attributes the problem of superficial coverage in part to textbooks. "Textbooks are the major medium for the coverage bacteria," said Newman, offering the opinion that high school teaching would vastly improve if the current texts were discarded.

In its report "Strategies for Achieving the National Education Goals," the National Governors' Association Task Force on Education concurred that it was critical for high schools to reduce their dependence on textbooks as the sole source of curriculum content. They recommended that states encourage the use of diverse instructional materials, including original sources, literature, and technology.

Schooling off track. Another practice that some scholars of American high schools have targeted for reform is that of tracking. Lezotte calls tracking "a force that distracts the school from its primary teaching-for-learning mission." Moreover, Lezotte said, "intended or not, many of the innovations that have been born from the 'excellence movement,' such as higher standards and stricter graduation requirements, are having the effect of increasing the sorting and selection function of the schools." The philosopher Mortimer Adler, in a collection of essays on educational reform, has also called for an end to tracking in high schools (as well as ability grouping in elementary grades).

Tracking continues to be widespread among American high schools. Many educators are reluctant to give up tracking because of its apparent practicality in responding to diverse student populations. School administrators surveyed by AASA for this document generally felt that most parents were opposed to the elimination of tracking and ability-grouping.

Yet, research indicates, one assumption on which tracking is based—that students learn better when grouped with students of similar ability—is problematic. A 1990 report of the Massachusetts Department of Education concluded that for the high school level, "most studies agree that approximately 60 percent of students not in top levels do suffer losses in academic achievement. In fact, one study found that students' I.Q. scores lowered following placement in lower levels."

The effects can be particularly damaging for poor and minority students. As the Massachusetts report noted, "The disproportionate numbers of poor and minority groups in lower-ability classes suggest that student differences are misunderstood and that individual strengths are overlooked when ability groups are formed. The segregation of poor and minority students does little to assist them: their placement in lower-ability classes denies them the opportunity to participate in the mainstream of education and achieve their full academic potential. In effect, ability grouping and tracking mirror and perpetuate social and economic inequalities."

The Need for More Research

Thomas B. Corcoran, education advisor to the governor of New Jersey and formerly with the Research for Better Schools laboratory in Philadelphia, says that the effective schools process offers great promise for the improvement of secondary education. He points to the fact, however, that only two studies have comprehensively analyzed secondary school effectiveness, and these studies had mixed results. One of the studies, which was conducted by University of Chicago sociologist James Coleman, was questioned because of its methodology.

Lawrence Lezotte, a founder of the effective schools process, also warned that there was "scant evidence of efforts to improve school learning climate. If we are to successfully meet the challenge of the failure of our low-income high schools . . . we must know more about the process of changing our secondary institution."

Corcoran points to some critical issues in secondary education that have generally been ignored by effective schools studies. These include:

- The impact of curricular paths, such as vocational, technical, scientific or artistic paths.
- Tracking.
- School size.
- The social context of secondary education.

There is a vast literature on each of these topics, says Corcoran, but few careful studies of the effect that variations in each factor have on general school success.

Fred Newman concurs that the issue of tracking is one that cannot be answered conclusively by existing research, in part because existing studies contain contradictory findings and in part because "the studies have not shown how the nature of instruction in different groups may actually affect student achievement indirectly, depending on what happens to students as they experience groups or tracks."

The conclusion that emerges from all of these voices is that more research, information, and models are needed to adapt the effective schools concepts to senior high schools.

Coalition of Essential Schools

One person who is trying to build a model for improving high schools is Theodore Sizer, backed up by the Coalition of Essential Schools. The Coalition grew out of a study of American secondary education conducted by Sizer from 1979 to 1984 and has the support of the National Association of Secondary School Principals, the National Association of Independent Schools, and the Education Commission of the States. "It really hurts me to say this," says Sizer,

A List of Common Principles for Essential High Schools

The Coalition of essential schools has developed a "List of Common Principles" based on the premise that the nation's high schools try to be too comprehensive and as a result impart only superficial knowledge. The principles are:

1. The school should focus on helping adolescents learn to use their minds well. Schools should not attempt to be 'comprehensive' if such a claim is made at the expense of the school's central intellectual purpose.

2. The school's goals should be simple: that each student master a limited number of essential skills and areas of knowledge.

3. The school's goals should apply to all students, even though the means of these goals will vary as those students themselves vary. School practice should be tailor-made to meet the needs of every group of students."

4. The student-teacher ratio ideally should be 13 or 14 students per teacher in each of six daily class periods in the present structure. Because of the expense such a proposition would entail, the Coalition would have teachers work as teams, in large time blocks, covering a variety of subjects: for example, an arts, humanities and language block, or a mathematics and sciences block. "Teachers would get to know their students better. Decisions about curriculum, allocation of time, and choice of teaching materials and their presentation must rest unreservedly with the school principal and staff.

5. The governing practical metaphor of the school should be student-as-worker, rather than the more familiar metaphor of teacher-as-deliverer of instructional services. Accordingly, a prominent pedagogy will be coaching, to provoke students to learn how to learn and thus to teach themselves.

6. The diploma should be awarded upon a successful final demonstration of mastery—an exhibition of the central skills and knowledge of the school's program. As the diploma is awarded when earned, the school's program proceeds with no strict age grading and with no system of 'credits earned' by 'time spent' in class.

7. The tone of the school should explicitly and self-consciously stress values of un-anxious expectation ('I won't threaten you but I expect much of you'), of trust (until abused) and of decency (the values of fairness, generosity and tolerance). Parents should be treated as collaborators.

8. The principal and teachers should perceive themselves as generalists first (teachers and scholars in general education) and specialists second (experts in but one particular discipline). Staff should expect multiple obligations (teacher-counselor-manager) and a sense of commitment to the entire school.

9. Ultimate administrative and budget targets should include, in addition to total student loads per teacher of 80 or fewer pupils, substantial time for collective planning by teachers, competitive salaries for staff and an ultimate per pupil cost not to exceed that spent at traditional schools by more than 10 percent. To accomplish this, administrative plans may have to show the phased reduction or elimination of some services provided in many comprehensive secondary schools."

The Coalition of Essential Schools

"but if you do anything you'll improve because there is almost no other effort out there to systematize improvement in our secondary schools."

With an awareness of effective schools research, Sizer has called for a different order of priorities in high school, characterized by lower student-teacher ratios and more resources per pupil.

Reordering priorities to Sizer means doing away with the traditional six-period day: giving up the tyranny of the bells. "How many adults," asks Sizer, "work for six bosses every day and change bosses every 40 to 45 minutes? Could you get your job done that way?"

"Coalition schools are about intellectual habit—habit of the mind. We reject the notion that facts once taught are learned. Instead, we place the emphasis on the student as active worker in the educational process, rather than as passive receiver of information," Sizer explained. "This approach requires a teacher to act as a coach, rather than a clerk checking off the number of subjects covered within the school year."

Reform Takes Time

According to Joan Shoemaker, director of school improvement for Connecticut and a fellow with the National Center for Effective Schools Research at the University of Wisconsin, implementing effective schools programs in high schools is a complex proposition that requires a significant, long-term commitment. It took Connecticut 10 years after its initial foray into the effective schools process to begin addressing improvement in the senior highs, said Shoemaker.

Accelerated Schools

Helping Children At Risk

A model for educating at-risk children developed by Henry Levin, a professor of education and economics at Stanford University, has taken a step further the precept of the effective schools movement that all children can learn. Levin believes the way to teach disadvantaged children is to "accelerate, not remediate." Says Levin: "What we need is a policy that accelerates learning for at-risk students, so that they will be academically able at an early phase of their schooling."

To meet the need, the Stanford Accelerated Schools Project, headed by Levin, has designed a model for accelerated elementary schools intended to help at-risk children catch up with their more advanced peers by the end of the sixth grade. "The entire school is dedicated to this objective," Levin explains, "and this commitment is reflected in the involvement of many participants. Teachers, parents, and students have high expectations, and set deadlines for students to meet particular educational requirements. The educational staff tailors the accelerated schools' instructional program to its students' needs. And the program uses all available resources in the community— including parents, senior citizens, and social service agencies."

At the heart of the effort is a commitment to build on the considerable strengths of its participants rather than censuring their weaknesses. The curriculum heavily emphasizes language throughout, even in mathematics, and introduces children early to the concepts of writing and reading for meaning. Problem-solving skills also are woven through the curriculum.

According to Levin, the approach he has developed not only raises achievement, but also reduces dropout rates, drug use and teenage pregnancies.

> **The way to teach disadvantaged children is to "accelerate, not remediate"**

Applying Correlates

Effective schools correlates play a role in accelerated schools. The principal is expected to be a strong instructional leader, and teachers and principals work in teams to improve the curriculum and make instructional decisions tailored to student needs. Teachers set high expectations for students; Levin's analogy is that "we must treat at-risk students in the same way that we treat all gifted and talented students." As well parental involvement is a key part of the program: parents are asked to sign a written agreement that clarifies their obligations and those of school staff and students. Parents also have opportunities to receive training in ways to assist and support their children.

Pilot Programs

A number of sites are operating around the country. The Stanford Project is overseeing experiments in the San Francisco Bay Area. Missouri and Illinois established statewide systems of accelerated schools in 1988 and 1989.

Parallel Block Scheduling

As noted earlier, an ongoing frustration among effective schools pioneers is the persistence of ability grouping and tracking in American schools. Nationally, somewhere between 77 and 88 percent of all schools use these practices. "The public is unwilling to accept schools that teach all children," posited Lawrence Lezotte. Some parents fear that heterogeneous grouping will slow down instruction for higher-ability students, leaving them bored and unchallenged. Others worry that at-risk students will fall farther and farther behind.

Mixed Groupings

Robert Lynn Canady, a professor at the University of Virginia with a background in effective schools research, has proposed an innovative approach for elementary schools that attempts to assuage these concerns by using a mixture of homogeneous and heterogeneous groupings during the school day and by establishing time for uninterrupted, small-group instruction for all students every day. The approach, called parallel block scheduling, is being used in more than 50 schools throughout the nation and represents a creative departure from traditional elementary school instruction.

In traditional small group instruction, Canady explains, pupils are sorted into groups; each group has its turn receiving instruction from the teacher, while the other groups do seat work. In parallel block scheduling, each teacher works with two groups. While one group receives instruction, the second group moves either to another classroom for support services or to an instructional area called an extension center—which can be located in the cafeteria, auditorium, media center, an extra classroom, or even a hallway—for a variety of enrichment activities, such as creative writing, computer lab, independent reading, and problem solving. The groups are not fixed; as topics change, students can be reassigned.

Benefits

Parallel block scheduling appears to have several advantages. It:

- increases the total amount of teacher-directed instructional time and does away with extensive periods of unsupervised seat work.
- eliminates the instructional interruptions and fragmentation that occur when children are pulled out of the regular classroom for special programs like Chapter 1 or bilingual education.
- ensures that support services are scheduled in a way that is convenient for both the classroom teacher and the resource teacher. and
- provides all students with equal instructional time in reading and mathematics.

Canady cited other advantages of parallel block scheduling:

- A lower student-teacher ratio. By alternating instruction, classroom teachers are able to spend about half the day working with

15 or fewer students.
- A reduction in the stigma of individual students being pulled out for special programs.
- Better mainstreaming of children with disabilities through an appropriate mixture of heterogeneous grouping for most instruction and homogeneous grouping for reading, mathematics, and special education (which makes it well suited for mainstreaming children with disabilities).
- Greater flexibility for staff assignments. According to Canady, studies of the education impacts of parallel block scheduling show that most students in schools using the approach, especially low-achieving children, seem to have higher achievement. And because students receive more teacher-directed instruction, time-on-task increases and discipline problems are reduced.

The model incorporates components of the effective schools planning process, by requiring principals and teachers to work closely in planning instruction for all students and requiring continuous reassessment of student progress. The model also calls for a schoolwide examination of instructional practices. "If genuine school reform is to occur," said Canady, "the most important changes must be made at the building level. High on the list of these changes is the redistribution of staff, space, and time within individual schools."

Additional Research and Development Needs

Leadership Training

The centrality of a strong leader to the effective schools process means that there is a constant need to train new leadership candidates and update the professional skills of present leaders. In a survey of AASA members, 62.2 percent of 726 respondents thought that pre-leadership training was a problem (although only 26.1 percent termed it a major problem).

With the exception of a limited number of federally-funded LEAD projects, most pre-leadership training is supported by local school districts.

Several unmet needs exist in leadership training. As the National Policy Board for Educational Administration noted, much of the training presently offered is largely irrelevant and does not prepare a future principal for daily school life, let alone leadership, in an effective school. The National Governors' Association Task

Force on Education also observed that "the inadequacy of programs to prepare principals and school superintendents is widely acknowledged; current programs offer administrators little grounding either in cognition and learning or in the modern principles of leadership and management."

Principals. Those who have closely studied leadership training programs suggest the need for updated curriculum, courses that focus on instructional leadership, collaborative decision-making, and procedures for evaluation and accountability. Researchers Thomas L. Good and Jere E. Brophy recommend that research on the principalship address the following issues:

- Whether a different type of principal is needed to improve a school's achievement rather than maintain an already adequate record;
- The role of the principal in assigning students and teachers to classes; and
- How principals influence instructional behavior in their schools.

Teachers. The effective schools approach demands a new type of teacher. Not all current teachers are adequately prepared to fill the roles assumed by the effective schools process. Inservice training is needed for current educators, and pre-service training is needed for the new cadre of people who will teach the children of the 21st century.

Minority teachers are particularly important presences in effective schools

A number of issues remain related to teacher training for effective schools. One is how to reorient current staff toward new instructional methods.

Another is how best to encourage talented young minority students to enter the teaching force. Minority teachers are particularly important presences in effective schools, all of which have an equity focus and many of which have large minority enrollments.

A third is how to mount meaningful staff development efforts for effective schools with limited resources.

A fourth is how to prepare teachers to cope with changing family structures, increased social stresses, and the growing demand for schools to take on more and more custodial responsibilities at the same time educators are trying to sharpen the focus on instruction.

Good and Brophy also suggest that research is needed on how the behavior of teachers in one school differs from that of teachers in another school, in such areas as homework assignments, use of drill, and development of independent study habits in students.

Assessment Issues

As discussed in Chapter 6, several questions remain about how best to measure school effectiveness. As Brian Rowan of the Far West Laboratory for Educational Research has concluded, "There is no consensus on which of the many standards and techniques for assessing instructional effectiveness is best. Instead, the choice of a particular procedure should be based on the purpose of the evaluation. A recommendation, however, is to devise procedures that construct longitudinal profiles of school academic performance at different grade levels, for different curricula, and for different sectors of the student body."

Lawrence Lezotte thinks it is time for "the gauntlet [to] be thrown down around the following standard: Did our students learn what we taught them in our program of curriculum and instruction?

If schools are going to move toward this standard of accountability, there will need to be a major change in the measures of school effectiveness. Schools will have to become less dependent on standardized, norm-referenced tests of achievement and, at the same time, increase their use of curriculum-based, criterion-referenced measures of pupil mastery," Lezotte said." If schools take seriously the curriculum-based and criterion-referenced measurement suggestion, the teachers and administrators will have to think much more broadly about the outcomes of instruction."

Conclusions. These comments suggest a research agenda that examines, at a minimum, the following issues regarding assessment in effective schools:

- New assessment tools, including performance-based instruments, need to be developed. Assessments that are objective, well suited to the correlates of effective schools, yet flexible enough to meet local needs, should be the aim.
- Tools for assessing outcomes in addition to achievement need to be created.
- Better techniques for analyzing student data and providing quicker feedback to teachers, perhaps using technology, need to be considered.
- The issue of alignment between curriculum and tests in effective schools could benefit from further study.
- Better measures of student and teacher perceptions need to be developed.

Other Research Questions

The research areas discussed above are by no means an exhaustive list. Experts have, for example, recommended further research in the following areas:

- The stability of effective schools (whether improved student achievement can be sustained across a period of years);
- Whether group averages accurately portray the effectiveness of individual teachers;
- The appropriate degree of teacher autonomy in effective schools;
- How to integrate various federal and state categorical programs into whole school improvement efforts; and
- Whether general studies of organizational theory and change processes have applications to effective schools.

The Legacy of the Effective Schools Movement

The effective schools movement is healthy and thriving. But even if, in a hypothetical world, all effective schools research was to halt abruptly, the movement would still have enormous ripple effects. One can scarcely underplay the impact of effective schools research on education reform during the past two decades. It has contributed concepts to the canon of school improvement that are now widely accepted by reform advocates, from philosopher Mortimer Adler to AFT President Albert Shanker. Among them are the following principles:

- Reform must come from the bottom up—from parents, teachers and administrators in individual schools—and must be an ongoing process. As a recent report from the Center for Policy Research in Education corroborated, it is the local efforts, not state or national plans, that are driving school reform.
- All children can learn, and schools can teach all children.
- Instructional approaches other than lecturing are more likely to foster genuine learning.
- Instructional approaches, such as ability grouping and tracking, that delegate certain groups of students to an inferior education or lower expectations are not appropriate, acceptable, or productive.

- Schools must be vigilant to keep the focus on their primary business of teaching and learning.
- Parents must become more involved in their child's education to enhance the child's success in school.

Epilogue

During the Korean War, a young Army captain in charge of a company of some 200 men was under heavy artillery fire to his front when he was ordered to lead a charge into the guns to save their lives. The captain disagreed with the order to attack and decided he would save his men by a quick retreat. Nearly all of his men were killed or wounded. The captain was severely hurt. When he recovered, he was court martialed, stripped of his rank and sent to prison. He was lucky. He could have been shot by a firing squad.

The lesson that the captain in the story learned is a lesson that many American educators have yet to learn, in the opinion of some scholars who have thought deeply about where American education should be heading. For years, say such thinkers as James Comer, Lawrence Lezotte, and Henry Levin, educators have been working from an assumption that there is only so much schools can do for certain groups of children. If the needs of these children were addressed at all, it was in the form of a scaled-down, slowed-down curriculum—a retreat, of sorts. Advocates of effective schools have attempted to turn around this situation by issuing a clarion call to teachers and school leaders. Push ahead, they say. Push harder and faster; do not ease up. Above all, do not retreat in the march toward better schools.

Sources

Adler, Mortimer J. *Reforming Education.* New York, N.Y.: Collier Books, MacMillan Publishing Company, 1990, pp. 131-135.

Albany, N.Y. *Monographs of Effective Schools.* New York State Council of Education Associations, Department of Research and Development.

Arasim, Liz; and Alex, Allie. *School Improvement: An Overview.* Lansing, Michigan: Michigan Senate Fiscal Agency, 1989, pp. 4-5.

Bossert, Steven T. "Effective Elementary Schools, Reaching for Excellence." Edited by Regina M. Kyle. *In An Effective Schools Sourcebook.* Washington, D.C.: Office of Educational Research and Improvement, U.S. Department of Education, July 1986, pp. 49, 50,51.

Boyer, Ernest L. "Education Goals: An Action Plan." Remarks at the National Governors' Association Winter Meeting, Washington, D.C., February 25, 1990.

Boyer, Ernest L. "School Reform: The Unfinished Agenda." Remarks before the Business Council, Hot Springs, Virginia, 1988.

Canady, Robert Lynn. "Parallel Block Scheduling: A Better Way to Organize a School." *Principal* (January 1990): pp. 34-36.

Corcoran, Thomas B. "Effective Secondary Schools. Reaching for Excellence." *In An Effective Schools Sourcebook.* Washington, D.C, U.S. Department of Education, Office of Educational Research and Improvement, July 1986, pp. 75,91,92.

Cornett, Lynn M. "Accountability in the SREB States." Paper presented to the annual meeting of the American Education Research Association, Boston, Massachusetts, 1990, pp. 3-10.

Council of Chief State School Officers. *Voices from Successful Schools: Elements of Improved Schools Serving At-Risk Students and How State Education Agencies Can Support More Local School Improvement.* Washington, D.C., 1990, pp. 29-35.

Council of the Great City Schools. *Results 2000: Progress in Meeting Urban Education Goals.* Washington, D.C., Fall 1990, p. 16.

Educational Research Service, for the American Association of School Administrators. *Opinions and Status of AASA Members,* 1988-89. Arlington, Virginia, January 1989. p. 16.

Elmore, Richard F. *Early Experiences in Restructuring Schools: Voices from the Field.* Washington, D.C.: National Governors' Association, 1988, pp. 16-19.

Firestone, W.; and Herriott, R. "Prescriptions for Effective Elementary Schools Don't Fit Secondary Schools." *Educational Leadership* 40, 3 (1982): pp. 51-53).

Gauthier, William J.; Pecheone, Raymond L.; and Shoemaker, Joan. "Schools Can Become More Effective." *Journal of Negro Education* 54, 3 (1985): pp. 388, 391-398.

Good, Thomas L.; Brophy, Jere E. "School Effects." Edited by Merlin C. Wittcock. *In Handbook of Research on Teaching.* New York: Macmillan, 1986, pp. 586-599.

Goodlad, John I. A *Place Called School: Prospects for the Future.* New York, N.Y.: 1984, (ED 236 137).

Gordon, Edmund W.; and Root, Leslie P.A. "Accelerated education can begin before kindergarten." Excerpts from their paper,"Pre-School Approaches to Accelerating the Education of At-Risk Students," presented at a conference in Stanford, California, 1989.

Hiebert, Elfredia H. "The Context of Instruction and Student Learning: An Examination of Slavin's Assumptions." Arlington, Virginia: American Education Research Association. Review of Educational Research 57, 3 (Fall 1987): pp. 337-340.

Houston, Robert W. (ed). The Handbook on Teacher Education. New York, N.Y.: MacMillan Publishing Co., 1990.

Levin, Henry M. "Don't Remediate: Accelerate." Excerpts from conference keynote address on "accelerating the education of at-risk students," Stanford, California, 1988.

Levine, Daniel U.; Lezotte, Lawrence W. *Unusually Effective Schools.* Madison, Wisconsin: National Center for Effective Schools, March 1990, pp. 71-71.

Lezotte, Lawrence W. *School Improvement Based on Effective Schools Research.* Okemos, Michigan, 1989, pp. 11-13.

Lezotte, Lawrence W. *Strategic Assumptions of the Effective Schools Process.* Okemos, Michigan, May 1988, pp. 1-3.

Lezotte, Lawrence W. *Alternative Images for School Improvement; Lezotte, L. W., et al. School Learning Climate and Student Achievement,* East Lansing, Michigan: Center for Urban Affairs, College of Education, Michigan State University. 1980, 1988.

Lockwood, Anne T. "To Track or Not To Track." An interview with Bruce Gregg, James Madison Memorial H.S., Madison, Wisconsin, National Center on Effective Secondary Schools. Newsletter (5) 1 (Spring 1990): pp. 10-11.

Massachusetts Board of Education. *Structuring Schools for Student Success: A Focus on Ability Grouping.* Boston, Massachusetts: January 1990, pp. 1,2,3,ll.

National Governors' Association. Task Force on Education Strategies for Achieving the National Education Goals. Washington, D.C., July 1990, pp 14,15,23,25,26,27,33,36,37,38,39,40

National Policy Board for Educational Administration. "Notes on Reform: State Certification Requirements for School Superintendents." University of Virginia, Charlottesville, Virginia, No. 7. 1989: pp.17-20.

Newman, Fred M. "Introduction." Madison, Wisconsin: National Center on Effective Secondary Schools. (5) l

Newman, Fred M., "Learning in High Schools." Madison, Wisconsin: Wisconsin State Research Association Journal. 33 (3) (Spring 1990): pp. 5-15.

Newman, Fred M. "Can Depth Replace Coverage in the High School Curriculum?" *Phi Delta Kappan,* January 1988, pp. 345-348.

Norris, Cynthia J.; Baptiste, Prentice; Weiss, Kay; and Macauluso, Lila. Paper presented to the American Educational Research Association, New Orleans, Louisiana, 1988, pp. 3-4.

Oakes, Jeannie. *Keeping Track: How Schools Structure Inequality.* New Haven, Connecticut: Yale University Press, 1985, ED 274 749.

Office of Educational Research and Improvement, U.S. Department of Education. *What's Happening in Teacher Testing? An Analysis of State Teacher Testing Practices.* Washington, D.C. 1987.

Olson, Lynn. "Goodlad on Teacher Education: Low Status, Unclear Mission." Washington, D.C.: *Education Week* (February 28,1990).

Purkey, S.C.; and Smith, M. "School Reform: The District Policy Implications of the Effective Schools Literature." *The Elementary School Journal* 85, 3 (1985): pp. 367-370.

"REACH: Realistic Educational Achievement Can Happen." Newsletter (1). Austin, Texas: Texas Education Agency, 1986, pp 1-2.

Rettig, Michael D.; Robert Lynn Canady. "Moving to the Right Side of the Tracks: Reducing School Structured Inequality Through Scheduling" (draft copy). Charlottesville, Virginia: The Curry School of Education, University of Virginia, July 1990.

Rowan, Brian. "The Assessment of School Effectiveness, Reaching for Excellence." *In An Effective Schools Sourcebook,* Edited by Regina M. Kyle. Washington, D.C.: OERI, July 1986, pp. 99, 102, 103, 106,114, 115.

Shanker, Albert. "Underestimating Children. Disadvantaged Doesn't Mean Dumb." New York: *The New York Times*, January 21, 1990.

Sizer, Ted. "Creating a Society That Thinks: Re: Learning." State Government News. The Council of State Governments, August 1988, pp. 20-21.

Sizer, Theodore, R. *Prospectus for the Coalition of Essential Schools.* Providence, Rhode Island: Brown University, 1985.

Sizer, Theodore, R. *Horace's Compromise: The Dilemma of the American High School.* Boston, Massachusetts: Houghton Mifflin, 1984.

Slavin, Robert E. *Achievement Effects on Ability Grouping in Secondary Schools: Best Evidence Synthesis.* Madison, Wisconsin: Clearinghouse, National Center on Effective Secondary Schools, 5 1 (1990).

Slavin, Robert E. "Ability Grouping and Student Achievement in Elementary Schools: A Best Evidence Synthesis." *Review of Educational Research.* Arlington, Virginia: American Educational Research Association, 57 3 (Fall 1987): pp. 293-336.

Slavin, Robert E.; Nancy A. Madden: "Instructional Strategies: What Works and What Doesn't." Excerpts from their paper, "Instructional Strategies for Accelerating the Education of At-Risk Students," presented at a conference on "accelerating the education of at-risk students" in Stanford, California.

"Southern Educators To Reassess School Accreditation Standards", *Education USA,* April 9, 1990, 32 (32). pp 239, 245.

Stallings, J.A.. "Program Implementation and Student Achievement in a Four-Year Madeline Hunter Follow-Through Project." *The Elementary School Journal.* 87, (1986): pp. 117-138.

Stallings, Jane A. *An Evaluation of the Napa County Office of Education's Follow Through Staff Development Effort To Increase Student Learning Time and Achievement.* Washington, D.C.: National Institute of Education. May 1985. (ED 245 303).

Stedman, Lawrence C. "It's Time We Changed the Effective Schools Formula." *Phi Delta Kappan.* (November 1987): p. 215.

U.S. House of Representatives. Public Law 100-297. Augustus F. Hawkins-Robert T. Stafford Elementary and Secondary School Improvement Amendments of 1988. 102 STAT 206-210.

Watkins, Beverly T. "Reform of Primary and Secondary Education Linked To Renewal of Teacher Training, Education Deans Are Told." Washington, D.C.: *The Chronicle of Higher Education,* Feb. 28, 1990.

A Self-Checklist for Principals

Instructional Leadership: Effective Behaviors

__ A. Do I take an active role in planning, conducting, implementing, and evaluating inservice training?
__ B. Do I provide direction and support for individual teachers to eliminate poor instructional performance?
__ C. Do I make sure the specifics of each teacher's classroom performance are evaluated?
__ D. Do I check carefully when hiring staff to ensure each will be effective to the students?

Instructional Leadership: Ineffective Behaviors

A. Does not provide effective feedback on instructional skills.
B. Denies importance of inservice programs.
C. Does not provide adequate classroom evaluation.
D. Hires teachers without an emphasis on teaching performance.
E. Does not require teaching improvement.

School Climate: Effective Behaviors

__ A. Do I personally enforce discipline with students?
__ B. Do I establish and enforce a clear code of conduct regarding rules such as attendance and absence policies?
__ C. Do I provide support and backup to enforce discipline?
__ D. Do I assign staff and resources to confront violations of established rules?
__ E. Do I create opportunities for staff to express ideas?
__ F. Do I listen "actively" to staff and faculty ideas?
__ G. Do I provide resources and a supportive environment for collaborative planning?
__ H. Do I establish school-wide goals and programs through staff proposals and participation?
__ I. Do I staff committees with representatives from all points of view—including views I disagree with —on a question or problem to be resolved?

School Climate: Ineffective Behaviors

A. Permits student behavior that creates a disorderly environment and disrupts classroom time.
B. Enforces discipline in a weak or inappropriate manner.
C. Does not establish and enforce a clear code of conduct, including attendance and absence policies.
D. Avoids enforcement of discipline and promotion of a studious atmosphere.
E. Avoids staff involvement in decisions or discussions.
F. Provides little or no feedback after meetings.
G. Does not support resources or support for collaborative planning.

High Expectations and Clear Goals: Effective Behaviors

__ A. Do I encourage students to pursue challenging academic goals?
__ B. Do I establish school-wide academic requirements?
__ C. Do I expect the counseling program to challenge students?
__ D. Do I set instructional standards for teachers?

High Expectations and Clear Goals: Ineffective Behaviors

A. Minimizes the importance of academic achievement in discussions with students.
B. Does not set specific goals for student performance.
C. Allows students (specifically in high schools) to get by with unchallenging student academic schedules.

Curriculum and Instruction: Effective Behaviors

__ A. Do I ensure that scope and sequence of curriculum exist and are adhered to?
__ B. Do I demonstrate knowledge and interest in each aspect of the curriculum?
__ C. Do I support teacher decisions and needs with action?
__ D. Do I provide staff with the atmosphere and resources to complete instructional tasks?

Curriculum and Instruction: Ineffective Behaviors

A Does not ensure scope and sequence exist and are being adhered to for each curriculum.
B. Does not provide administrative support for curricular problems.
C. Denies teachers supplies and resources through misadministration.
D. Displays a lack of confidence and respect for teachers.
E. Makes unreasonable demands on teachers outside of teaching responsibilities.

Testing and Student Recognition: Effective Behaviors

__A. Do I make special efforts, in addition to regular ongoing award programs, to give visibility and high quality recognition for academic achievement?
__B. Have I set up continuous programs for recognition of academic success?
__C. Do I encourage the use of standardized testing for student academic performance? Do I weigh standardized tests as one of several ways to measure success? Do I take the various methods into account for grading purposes?
__D. Do I give personal recognition to individual students for their specific academic achievements?

Testing and Student Recognition: Ineffective Behaviors

A. Mishandles student recognition.
B. Ignores or misuses standardized tests.

Parental Support: Effective Behaviors

__A. Do I seek active parental involvement in school activities?
__B. Do I communicate on a regular basis with parents of individual students?
__C. Do I inform parents of special programs and activities?
__D. Do I interact directly with parents and others in the community to promote the school?
__E. Do I make special efforts to direct personal contacts between parents and teachers?

Parental Support: Ineffective Behaviors

    A. Avoids interpersonal communications with parents.
    B. Communicates in a manner that will make parents angry
       or feel negative toward the school.
    C. Discourages parental involvement.
    D. Succumbs to nonacademic interest groups.
    E. Does not meet with parents on positive topics.

Principal and Selection Guide: A Blueprint for Excellence

Self-Checklist for Superintendents

    Superintendents also have a responsibility to assess their own effectiveness. The following questions were drawn from two AASA publications: *Selecting a Superintendent,* a joint publication of AASA and the National School Boards Association, and *The Role of the Principal* by Jack McCurdy.

A Self-Checklist for Superintendents

__ Do I consider myself the school board's chief executive officer?
__ Do I serve as the board's professional adviser in all manners?
__ Do I recommend without fear or trepidation appropriate school policies for the board's consideration?
__ Once the school board sets the policy, do I move to implement it without delay?
__ Do I make sure the board members and their staff are fully and accurately informed about the school programs?
__ Do I interpret the needs of my school system to the board with clarity? (Does everyone understand me?)
__ Do I present my professional recommendations on all problems and issues for the board's consideration?
__ Do I arrange to consult with my principals on a scheduled basis?
__ How often do I visit schools in my district?
__ Do I devote my major thoughts and time to the improvement of instruction?
__ How do I establish criteria for evaluating the educational program?

__ Am I alert to the latest advances and improvements in educational programs wherever they can be found?

__ How have I improved the school system I am now directing?

__ How would I improve the abilities of the professional staff?

__ Am I leading in the development and operation of a school community relations program?

__ Do I understand the politics and personalities within my community with an eye on enlisting their support for my schools?

__ Have I been successful in gaining support from voters for levies and bond issues?

__ How much care do I take in nominating candidates for school staff?

__ Have I been appropriately involved in collective bargaining?

__ Do I listen, examine and consult with the variety of factions in my community before I present an annual budget designed to meet the system's needs?

__ Have I identified which federal and state educational programs are most significant for my district?

__ Do I supervise the financial operations of my school district to ensure adherence to budget?

__ Is student learning and development my bottom line?

Self-Checklist for School Board Members

The National School Boards Association has developed a self-examination checklist for school board members. Some of the questions are relevant to effective schools and strong leadership.

A Self-Checklist for School Board Members

__ What should your board do for your school district? What should your board do that it does not do now?

__ What changes has your district undergone in the past five years, 10 years, 20 years? What changes do you anticipate in the next two years, five years, 10 years? What plans are being made to manage these changes?

___ What are your district's major objectives this year and next?

___ How does your board go about setting goals and objectives for the district? What planning procedures does it follow?

___ If your district could obtain one major objective next year, what would you want it to be? If the board agrees with you, does it have a plan that would accomplish it? If not, who can help you devise and implement such a plan?

___ When was the last time your board reviewed its policies?

___ How does your board know whether its policies are implemented in the schools?

___ Is your district managed by an administrative team? If so, who is on it? How does it function? How does your board interact with it?

___ How does your board evaluate administrative efforts?

___ How are school programs evaluated?

___ What staff development opportunities are provided to school employees?

___ How does your board influence the curriculum?

___ What can you do personally to help ensure good working relationships between yourself and the superintendent and staff?

___ Does your district have citizen advisory committees? What do they do?

___ How does your board respond to complaints from citizens? What should you do when a citizen complains to you about a school-related matter?

HIEBERT LIBRARY

3 6877 00195 8940

ACKNOWLEDGMENTS

LB
2822.82
.B43
1992

AASA is grateful to the school administrators who took the time to answer the survey questionnaire about effective schools.

Special thanks go to Lawrence Lezotte, Kent Peterson, Joan Shoemaker and Barbara Taylor at the National Center for Effective Schools; Fred M. Newman, director of the National Center on Effective Secondary Schools; Susan Traiman of the National Governors' Association; Theodore Sizer of Brown University; Paul Soder of the University of Washington, Seattle; Gordon Davies, chairman of the Virginia Council of Higher Education; Robert Hochstein of the Carnegie Foundation for the Advancement of Teaching; John Hollifield at the Johns Hopkins University Center for Research in Elementary and Middle Schools; Robert Blum of the Northwest Regional Development Laboratory; Robert Wimpelberg of the University of New Orleans; Robert Canady of the University of Virginia; June Million of the National Association of Elementary School Principals; and Lewis Armistead of the National Association for Secondary School Principals.

Also included on the list of helpful sources is Ann Madison of Norfolk Public Schools; Louise Wynant and Jeff Schiller of the Prince George's County, Maryland, Schools; Marc Becker of the Glendale, Arizona, School District; Tom Fitzgerald, bureau chief for school improvement for the State of New York; Milton Goldberg, director of research at the U.S. Department of Education; and Oliver Moles and Marshall Saskin, senior research associates in OERI.

An Effective Schools Primer was written by former U.S. Department of Education Communications Staff member Myron Becker, with the editorial assistance of Nancy Kober, education writer; AASA Senior Associate Executive Director Gary Marx, who served as project director; and AASA Editors Barbara M. Bell and Leslie Eckard. The book was designed by Sans Serif Graphics.